W9-BXT-232

ONE FOR THE GRAVE

By the same author

*

DRAMA

The Dark Tower

Christopher Columbus

Out of the Picture

The Mad Islands and *The Administrator*

*

POETRY

The Collected Poems of Louis MacNeice

Selected Poems

The Burning Perch

Solstices

Visitations

Autumn Journal

Autumn Sequel

Springboard

The Other Wing (*Ariel Poem*)

*

TRANSLATION

The Agamemnon of Aeschylus

Goethe's Faust (*Parts I and II*)

with E. L. Stahl

*

AUTOBIOGRAPHY

The Strings are False: An Unfinished Autobiography

One for the Grave

a modern morality play

by

LOUIS MACNEICE, 1907-1963

New York
OXFORD UNIVERSITY PRESS
1968

Printed in Great Britain

PREFATORY NOTE

This play was written by Louis MacNeice in 1958–9. It is unrevised and is here printed as he left it.

The world premiere was given at the Abbey Theatre during the Dublin Theatre Festival, 1966. The director was Frank Dermody; the settings were by Liam Miller and the music by Gerard Victory.

The cast was as follows:

FLOOR MANAGER	Bill Foley
DIRECTOR	Vincent Dowling
SECRETARY	Bernadette McKenna
DESIGNER	Alec Doran
JIMMY (Studio Hand)	Michael O'Briain
VISION MIXER	Chris O'Neill
CROONER	Des Cave
LIL	Geraldine Plunkett
EVERYMAN	Pat Layde
MAGGIE	Eileen Crowe
ELEANOR	Kathleen Barrington
LOVER	Patrick Laffan
CAREER	Edward Golden
A CADDY	Niall Buggy
CONSCIENCE	Brenda McGuinne
LUCRE	Geoffrey Golden
COMMON SENSE	Phil Cahill
SON	Donal McCann
DAUGHTER	Maire O'Neill
DOREEN	Deirdre Purcell
MARY	Sinead Cusack
FORGETFULNESS	Sheila O'Connell

MOTHER	Joan O'Hara
SACRIFICE	Eileen Lemass
PATRIA	Aideen O'Kelly
ADMOM	Maire Ni Dhomhnaill
ELECTRONIC BRAIN	Des Cave
SEAN BULL	Peadar Lamb
COMEDIAN	Alice Dalgarno
FREE WILL	Donal McCann
ANALYST	Michael O hAonghusa
MARXIST	Stephen Rea
SCIENTIST	Patrick Laffan
SINGER	Angela Newman
DR. DIVINITY	Philip O'Flynn
DR. MEDICINE	Peadar Lamb
GRAVEDIGGER	Geoffrey Golden
CAMERAMAN NO. 1	John Kelly
CAMERAMAN NO. 2	Michael O hUannachain
BOOM OPERATOR	John Horgan
STUDIO HAND	Phelim O'Donnell
POP SINGERS	Jack Daly, J. McKay, Louis Stewart

Also as many stage hands, members of camera crews, wardrobe and make-up types, etc. etc., as can be afforded and accommodated on the stage. Also voices off—both speaking and singing.

CHARACTERS

The Floor Manager
The Director
His Secretary
The Designer
The Crooner
A Cameraman
Jimmy (a props man)
Everyman
Maggie
Eleanor
Her Lover
Career
A Caddy
Conscience
Lucre
Common Sense
The Son
The Daughter
Doreen
Mary
Forgetfulness
The Mother
The Vision Mixer
Sacrifice
Patria
Admom
The Electronic Brain
Sean Bull
The Comedian
Free Will
The Analyst
The Marxist
The Scientist
Lil (a dresser)
The Gravedigger
The Doctor of Med
The Doctor of Div

NOTES

1. N.B. This is still very much a *draft*, to which much could be added and/or subtracted. Indeed this piece should always remain to *some* extent elastic if only in order to stay up to date: unlike its medieval model, the topical allusions are important.

2. The basic pattern, however, the story line, follows that of the medieval Everyman and must on no account be sacrificed. This means that in production a very delicate balance must be preserved between its primary content, which is serious, and the revue or music hall elements (sometimes pretty near slapstick) which are introduced not primarily for their own sake but for satirical purposes, the modern Everyman's world being one which cannot be properly treated *without* satire.

3. This being so the whole device of the Television Studio (where the floor represents the Earth and the production gallery Heaven) is very much more than a gimmick —because it is the fate of the twentieth-century Everyman to live in a world of mass media. Similarly, the Admom sequence is not just there for comic relief.

4. As regards casting: the actor playing Everyman must obviously be extremely plastic, changing tint at the drop of a hat. The Son and Daughter must also be versatile. The Floor Manager should superficially resemble a quite usual type of suave (perhaps slightly Americanized) light entertainment F.M. but with an undertone of sinister authority. As for the Director, his face must never be seen and he should move as little as possible, except perhaps for the well-known flick of thumb and fingers when ordering a cut. He requires a deep and dominating voice.

5. Acting: Obviously the style will vary between the naturalistic flashback scenes and the stylized ones. In the latter, especially during musical numbers, the various stage hands, etc., on the studio floor should, in grouping and movement, be treated like the rank-and-file members of a revue.

6. Spectacle: This obviously depends on (*a*) the size of stage and (*b*) what funds are available. While the play *could* be done in a token way, the more the production can suggest the bustle of a real TV studio with its crowds of personnel and clutter of machines (e.g. the boom—a most spectacular prop) the better. By the way, the audience represents an invited *television* audience.

7. Music: At the moment many of the lyrics are set to traditional tunes: I should like this kept in most cases but all such should be arranged and, if necessary, modernized by the same hand that sets the deliberately modern numbers. Some could be unaccompanied, but a small (modern) ensemble or, at any rate, one or two *popular* instruments will be required for others. If necessary, the choirs off could be canned.

L.M.

ACT ONE

Lights up on front of empty stage, which represents a television studio. On stage a token tracking camera on wheels with a small platform which ideally should be able to be raised or lowered for cameraman, and a rail behind for one man to push it. Also, ideally, a boom—which again would involve two men—but this is not strictly essential. Upstage—but, ideally, more or less blacked out to start with—three small shallow sets of TV type, numbering I to III from Stage L. to R.: if a revolve is available, it would be better to have these three sets on it so that only one shows at a time. Two entrances L. and R. with red lights over them spelling EXIT. Upstage on an upper level or bridge, but blacked-out to start with, the Production Gallery—? screened by gauze—where the DIRECTOR *and his assistants sit with their backs to the audience: facing the audience there should be a suggestion of a line of monitors.*

When the lights are fully up, the FLOOR MANAGER*'s voice is heard shouting, off.*

FLOOR MANAGER: Come on, chaps! Get on the floor! The audience is waiting.

(*From both entrances there pour in a number of technicians, studio hands, etc., who take up their respective positions. The* FLOOR MANAGER *follows, in a dinner jacket with headphones draped round his neck, and comes downstage to address the audience.*)

FLOOR MANAGER: Ladies and gentlemen, good evening. Welcome to our theatre! I'm glad to see you all looking so fit. You'll need to be for this show.

DIRECTOR'S VOICE (*on slight distort, out of darkness*): Get on with it, Morty. Cut the wisecracks.

Floor Manager: Sorry, chief. Well, ladies and gentlemen, I expect most of you have been in a television theatre before, but for the benefit of those who haven't let me just put you in the picture. (*Stamps.*) This . . . is the floor of the studio and I am the floor manager. Familiarly called the F.M. Or, putting it another way, I always have my feet on the earth. But, to put out a show, we need more than the earth—the floor. We need the powers up above.

(*Lights up Production Gallery, showing back of Director seated between two or more figures—? dummies—whom he should overtop.*)

Look up there. That is the Production Gallery. That's where the Director sits.

(Director *raises his hand in backward salute.*)

With him are his Secretary, his Vision Mixer and others. The whole show is controlled from that gallery and the Director's word is absolute.

Director's Voice: When it can be heard, Morty.

Floor Manager: He said 'when it can be heard'. The Director has a sense of humour. Well, there you have it: the Gallery up there is Olympian remoteness—

(*Black-out Gallery.*)

and the Floor down here where we all have our feet on the earth: camera crews, props men, all of us—and of course the artists. But no doubt you're wondering how the floor and the gallery keep in touch? It's simple. (*Put on headphones.*) You see these headphones—or cans as we call them in the trade! Through these I can hear whatever the Director says. Like this. Hullo, Chief! Can you hear me?

Director's Voice: What was that, Morty?

Floor Manager: Sorry, Chief: can't hear you.
Director's Voice: I said: What was that?
Floor Manager: I only said: Can't you hear me?
Director's Voice: Only just. You'll have to speak up.
Floor Manager: Okay Chief. I told you it was simple, didn't I. The Director up there speaks into a talkback and I hear what he says on these cans and I pass on his orders to the studio. Though, as you'll have noticed, there are one or two other people who also wear cans —like our Number One cameraman there and that other chap up there with that thing like a giant steel fishing-rod; that's what we call the boom, it's got a mike on the end of it. To both these chaps the Director can speak direct but to most of the others he has to speak through *me*. And it's I who keep them on their toes. Well, now I think I've put you in the picture but, before we start the show, I'd just like to ask you all a favour. This is an actuality show and our leading actor is an amateur, so when you're watching it please don't only watch it entertainmentwise; please watch it also imaginationwise. Point taken? Excellent. (*He turns away.*)
Director's Voice: Morty! You've forgotten Admom. (Floor Manager *turns back to audience.*)
Floor Manager: Ladies and gentlemen, I'm terribly sorry. Before the show starts I want to introduce to you one of your favourite artists, who will entertain you at the interval. You all must have seen her many times; to some of you she's a mother, to some of you she's a sweetheart, to some of you she's no less than a great big guardian angel. (*He cues towards the nearer entrance.*) Ladies and gentlemen, your very own Admom!

(ADMOM *enters, to fanfare. Flashy middle-aged glamour—blend of brass and sugar. She blows kisses to audience.*)

She's saving her voice for later, but you see what a treat's in store for you. Okay, Chief. Blackout the studio!

(*Blackout stage; light Gallery.*)

DIRECTOR: What's wrong, Pam?

SECRETARY (*facing him and audience*): This script.

DIRECTOR: Well, what about it?

SECRETARY: It's blank. Not a line of dialogue in it.

DIRECTOR: Pam dear! How long have you been my secretary? Haven't you taken in yet we're not televising a *play*! This show is pure actuality.

SECRETARY: Then I don't have to call the shots?

DIRECTOR: Of course not. Just sit in your place and take any notes I give you.

(*She sits beside him.*)

Now where's that designer?

SECRETARY: He was down on the floor just now putting some last minute touches——

(DESIGNER *comes in, facing audience.*)

DIRECTOR: Ah there you are, Julian!

DESIGNER: Sorry if I've held things up. Some of the props were wrong, as usual. They'd delivered a lot of medieval ones. Memento mori stuff.

DIRECTOR: Oh these wretched supply departments! When it *was* the Middle Ages, they were always sending us shooting sticks.

DESIGNER: And Sten guns sometimes.

DIRECTOR: And Sten guns. Okay, Morty! Ready in the studio?

FLOOR MANAGER (*on distort, from darkness*): We're ready.

Camerawise, lightingwise, boomwise, artwise, lifewise, and deathwise.

DIRECTOR: Good. Then we'll go from the top. Silence in the studio.

(*Blackout Gallery: light Studio.*)

FLOOR MANAGER: Silence in the studio! Stop that damned racket! We're going from the top. Jimmy, bring that mike further down.

(*A studio hand brings handmike downstage.* FLOOR MANAGER *cues the nearer entrance.* CROONER *comes in and advances briskly to mike.*)

CROONER (*crooning*): On earth—
For what it's worth—
We meet
And part—
Oh my baby-blue blushpink battleship-grey life!
We meet
In the street,
We part
In the cart,
We live
Like a spiv,
We die
Like a fly,
For what it's all consumerwise actionwise
inactionwise bodywise brainwise heartwise
soulwise creationwise damnationwise worth—
On earth . . .
For what it's worth.

DIRECTOR'S VOICE: Come on; grams there! Clapping!

(*Clapping on discs;* CROONER *bows and goes off.*)

That could have been smoother but we can't go back

on it. Can't go back on anything tonight. They all know that, don't they, in the studio?

FLOOR MANAGER: The boys all know it. Perhaps I ought to tell the audience. (*Comes downstage.*) Ladies and gentlemen, before our leading actor comes on, perhaps there's one more thing I should explain to you. This is really a very peculiar sort of show because it's not a finished product—and never will be. In fact it's really a rehearsal but it's not a typical rehearsal because . . . well, there's only one of it. It's a sort of do-it-yourself job and the man who does it is Everyman. And now I'm going to cue him.

DIRECTOR'S VOICE: Hold it, Morty! Camera One, are you focused on that entrance?

(CAMERAMAN *holds up hand in assent.*)

What lens angle are you on?

CAMERAMAN: Zero.

DIRECTOR: Okay. It's yours, Morty.

(FLOOR MANAGER *cues.* EVERYMAN *enters, bang opposite camera. He is middling well dressed and might come from any sphere of society.* FLOOR MANAGER *cues him again. He does not speak.*)

FLOOR MANAGER: Come on, come on! Your lines!

EVERYMAN: But I haven't learnt them.

FLOOR MANAGER: Boy! You've left it late!

EVERYMAN: They told me this was actuality. I thought it must be some sort of quiz programme.

FLOOR MANAGER: Everyman, you're right there. Only this is a universal quiz.

EVERYMAN: Universal?

FLOOR MANAGER: Any time, any place, common or garden, ultimate. After all, my dear fellow, this is a mass medium. Look, I'll brief you quickly. The Director of this show is high up there—you can't see him—so it's I that relays his directions to the artists.

EVERYMAN: But I'm not an artist; I've never even been in a studio before.

FLOOR MANAGER: In *this* studio you have. Light up that first set.

(*Light up Set One—a token luxury flat with sofa and academic pictures. It is empty.*)

Remember that room?

EVERYMAN (*dreamily*): Oh yes . . . yes. . . . But I've just come from there. Eleanor was sitting on that very sofa beside me. But where's she gone?

FLOOR MANAGER: It's *you* who've gone. Okay. Set Two.

(*Blackout Set One: light Two—a mean little office with a typewriter on the desk and a sheet of paper protruding from it.*)

EVERYMAN: But I've just come from there too! I was typing a memo, I think. Only what was it about? It's funny, I——

FLOOR MANAGER: Bring it over here, Bill.

(BILL *extracts memo and brings it downstage to* FLOOR MANAGER.)

FLOOR MANAGER: 'M. . . . You never finished it. Shall I jog your memory? The last sentence begins: (*reads*) 'In view of the above considerations and particularly this matter of my failing health I feel reluctantly compelled, in spite of my loyalty to the firm, or perhaps I should say because of it, to tender my. . . .' That's where you stuck. I presume you meant 'resignation'.

EVERYMAN: Did I? Nonsense! I never meant to resign.

FLOOR MANAGER: No? Set Three!

(*Blackout Set Two, light Three—a slum bedroom.*)

EVERYMAN (*with changed accent*): Oh there? Never want to go there again!

(*A woman half-rises from the bedclothes.*)

MAGGIE: Evvy! Is that you? Come back at once!

FLOOR MANAGER: Quick change here. Wardrobe!

(*Wardrobe whips off Everyman's jacket and tie.*)

Up you go! She needs you.

(EVERYMAN, *as if doped, goes upstage and on to Set Three and sits gingerly on a cane chair.*)

MAGGIE: No Evvy! Closer.

(*He shuffles chair up to bed.*)

Well, can't you kiss your own wife?

EVERYMAN: No, Maggie, I can't.

MAGGIE: Course you can't! You feel too guilty. (*Silence.*) Not much to say for yourself, have you?

EVERYMAN: What have you to say for *me*?

FLOOR MANAGER: Right cue for once. Tell him.

MAGGIE: Why should I say anything for him?

FLOOR MANAGER: Because he's about to die.

MAGGIE: Oh is he indeed! Well, before he dies, here's an earful for him.

EVERYMAN: Who said I was about to——

MAGGIE: Shut up! You know what you done to me, Evvy. Married me on false pretences and dragged me down and down. Oh it wasn't just you called yourself a clerk when you was only common working class. And it wasn't just the horses and the drinks and the tarts——

EVERYMAN: There wasn't no tarts.

MAGGIE: Oh wasn't there! But it wasn't just the debts all them things led to, it was the way you withered. And withered me up along with you. When I think of that first time as you took me out to the flicks and your eyes had a lovelight in 'em as good as what was on the screen like and when I compares you then with what you become now——

EVERYMAN: It was your fault just as much as mine.

FLOOR MANAGER: Wrong answer!

(*Gong. Blackout Set Three.*)

Wardrobe! His jacket and tie.

(*They are carried upstage.*)

DIRECTOR'S VOICE: Nice work there, all the cameras.

(CAMERAMAN *raises hand.* EVERYMAN *returns downstage in jacket and tie, bemused.*)

FLOOR MANAGER: Ready to go on?

EVERYMAN: No. What was that Maggie said? About me dying?

FLOOR MANAGER: I said it.

EVERYMAN: But only in the play?

FLOOR MANAGER: I've told you it isn't a play.

EVERYMAN: Anyway that wasn't me. (*Changes accent.*) The real me was over there. (*Points.*)

FLOOR MANAGER: Set One!

(*Lights Set One*—ELEANOR *on sofa, weeping.*)

EVERYMAN: Eleanor! But why's she crying?

FLOOR MANAGER: For you—we must assume.

(*Eleanor's lover comes in, kisses her and sits down close to her.*)

LOVER: Not still crying, darling? But you know you didn't love him.

ELEANOR: No . . . but I was fond of him.

LOVER: Of course you were. However, now we can get married.

ELEANOR: I know; it's freedom for both of us. But if only

it had come a shade. . . .

LOVER: Sooner?

ELEANOR: Later. Look, darling, I'll be candid; it's a sordid matter of death duties. He knew he had a heart, you see, so he made a settlement in my favour—one of those five years arrangements. Well, this is the fifth year but there still are two months to run.

(*The* LOVER *draws away from her.*)

Damn him, damn him, damn him! Why did he always bungle everything?

(*Blackout Set Three.*)

FLOOR MANAGER: You see? You're damned there too. (*Looks at wristwatch.*) 'M. We're running a shade slow.

EVERYMAN (*to self*): No, there was never any future in it; I must have known that all along. Still, I didn't know she had a lover.

FLOOR MANAGER: No future in it, did you say? You don't mean a future life?

EVERYMAN: I don't know anything about that.

FLOOR MANAGER: Don't you?

EVERYMAN: Do *you*?

FLOOR MANAGER: I'm not here to answer questions: I'm here in charge of this studio. It's you who must answer any questions there are. And I tell you time's running short.

EVERYMAN: I think my life here is possibly the only one.

FLOOR MANAGER: Possibly?

EVERYMAN: Probably.

FLOOR MANAGER: Not 'certainly'?

EVERYMAN: Probably.

FLOOR MANAGER: Then let's assume it is the only one. In that case, has it been worth while?

EVERYMAN: Of course it's been worth while.

MAGGIE'S VOICE (*from darkness*): Liar!

EVERYMAN: Don't listen to her. I told you that wasn't me.

ELEANOR'S VOICE (*from darkness*): Liar!

EVERYMAN: Don't listen to her either. You can't pin me down like this. After all I'm Everyman. I've had wives and lives by the million, I've had every sort of career, I've——

DIRECTOR'S VOICE: Cue Career! Camera One, stand by for a two-shot.

(FLOOR MANAGER *cues.* CAREER *enters, dressed like a Civil Servant, attended by a caddy with a large golf bag full of various implements.*)

EVERYMAN: Career! Just the chap I wanted to see! I need your help in a new transaction; I'm relying on you to guarantee——

CAREER: Guarantee what exactly?

EVERYMAN: Me!

CAREER: You, my dear Everyman? Well, it depends whether you're talking of means or ends——

FLOOR MANAGER: Make it the singular; call it 'end'.

EVERYMAN: Help me, Career. Look, you're my friend——

CAREER:

Yes, but I have to know in advance
What it is you propose to do:
(*Very fast.*)
To build a new town or destroy an old
Or found a college or a zoo
Or turn a screw or dissect a mouse
Or launch a rocket or sell a pup
Or breed a rose or delouse a louse
Or train a team for the Davis Cup

Or chart the stars on screen or sky
Or manage a bank or write an ad
Or cook an account or an oyster pie
Or make a film of 'The Shropshire Lad'
Or gather plankton from the brine
Or drill for oil or lift a face
Or start one more uranium mine
Or operate on a hopeless case
Or conduct a bus or a five-piece band
Or design a dam or an atom pile—
For any of these I'm here at hand,
Ready to help you with a smile.

EVERYMAN:
Thank you, Career. I must reply
It's none of these—and you know why?
What I propose to do is die.

CAREER: Then I can't help you.

EVERYMAN:
But you can!
You are Career and I am man.
I call upon you to confirm
That I was worth that waste of sperm
And that this curious thing we call
Life is a good thing after all.
Therefore, before I keep my date
With tight-lipped and tight-fisted Fate,
I ask you to corroborate
That here on earth I pulled my weight.

CAREER: Caddy! The putter!
(CADDY *hands* EVERYMAN *a putter.*)

CAREER: Your weight with this?
(EVERYMAN *makes a feeble stroke with it, towards*

audience, at an invisible ball: then with an air of despondency hands it to a stage hand. CAREER *takes telescope from Caddy and hands it to Everyman.*)

CAREER: Or this?

(EVERYMAN *looks through telescope over audience, shakes his head sadly and hands it over.* CAREER *hands him a Sten gun.*)

CAREER: Or this?

(EVERYMAN *passes it on hastily.* CAREER *hands him a set of sweep's rods.*)

CAREER: Or this?

(EVERYMAN *tries to fit them together, makes an upward lunge—and they fall apart. He hands them over.* CAREER *hands him a bishop's crozier.*)

CAREER: Or this?

(EVERYMAN *holds it in his left hand, makes as if to bless audience with his right, then shakes his head and hands it over.* CAREER *hands him a bass clarinet.*)

CAREER: Or this?

(EVERYMAN *puts his mouth to it and with great effort produces one hideous sound. He passes it on.* CAREER *hands him a rolled umbrella.*)

CAREER: Or this?

(EVERYMAN *for some time examines umbrella as if he didn't know what it was, then suddenly smiles a smile of recognition, unrolls it very deliberately, puts it up and stands under it.*)

CAREER: Why are you silent, Everyman?

FLOOR MANAGER: Strike that umbrella. His face is not in camera.

(*A stage hand removes the umbrella.*)

Well? He asked you why you are silent.

EVERYMAN. Then I ask *him*. All these and more
I used in life, but let *him* tell——
Tell them, Career—I used them well.

CAREER: Oh yes, at times—at others not.
You used them certainly—but for what?
(*A pansy male figure,* LUCRE, *and a female figure,* CONSCIENCE, *have suddenly appeared.*)

CAREER: For which of these? For him? For her?

EVERYMAN: These two? They're two I've never met.

CONSCIENCE:
You have met me. Can you forget!
When you were young and first began
To work, whatever work it was
You yearned to prove yourself a man
Or else to help your fellow men
Or both perhaps at once, because
You had some inkling of me then.

EVERYMAN: I'm sorry—but I have none now.
(*Gong.*)

FLOOR MANAGER: Point taken. Tell him why and how.

CONSCIENCE:
My name is Conscience. You, when young,
Knew me a little—not for long—
And then you met this fellow here
Who called your tune for many a year.

EVERYMAN: He certainly didn't!

LUCRE: Yes, I did.
Don't you remember in Madrid
Turning your coat in '36
And not because of politics—
Oh no, my dear, because of me.
And don't you remember other years

In other countries, other spheres—
The League of Nations, the T.U.C.,
In art or sport or God knows what
Selling the pass, selling the lot,
And at a bargain—you agree?
Since what you lost was only she
And what you won was none but me.

EVERYMAN: Then you are. . . ?

LUCRE: Lucre.

(*Gong.*)

EVERYMAN: Lucre!

LUCRE: Yes, my dear, they call me 'filthy'—but that's only their fun, you know.

(*He takes out a compact and powders his nose. A* BELL-BOY *comes in with a cablegram on a salver.*)

BELL-BOY: Paging Filthy Lucre! Paging Filthy Lucre! etc.

LUCRE: Here I am. (*Opens cablegram.*) I must fly! They want me at a summit conference. (*Goes out.*)

CONSCIENCE (*to audience*): And me? Who wants me?

DIRECTOR'S VOICE: Morty! Get her off.

(FLOOR MANAGER *cues Conscience to exit.*)

And Career too.

(FLOOR MANAGER *cues Career.*)

CAREER: Good-bye, Everyman.

EVERYMAN: Wait a minute.

CAREER: I can't.

EVERYMAN: Just a minute.

CAREER (*indicating* FLOOR MANAGER): He won't let me.

(*He goes out.*)

FLOOR MANAGER: Over to you, Everyman. He let you down, didn't he? Better try another witness.

EVERYMAN (*northern accent, ponderingly*): Another witness?

Where's my thinking cap?
(*Wardrobe puts cloth cap on Everyman.*)
Nay, Career were no cop. Ah'd trust my Common Sense though. Where is t'lass?
(FLOOR MANAGER *cues into wings. A female figure enters, plainly and severely dressed, wearing secretarial spectacles.*)

EVERYMAN: Hullo, luv. Ah knew tha'd come on tick.

COMMON SENSE: Everyman, what's wrong now?

EVERYMAN: Wrong! Nowt's reet. Ah'm on spot, luv.

COMMON SENSE: What spot?

EVERYMAN: Ah'm due for coffin.

COMMON SENSE: Well, don't let them charge you too much for it.

EVERYMAN: That's not what ah mean. Ah want thy services as witness for defence.

COMMON SENSE: Do you indeed? And what do you expect me to say?

EVERYMAN: Summat like this. Ah want thee to say Ah always used thee proper and followed all thy advice in matters both great and small——

COMMON SENSE: I'll say nothing of the sort. Followed my advice indeed! When I warned you not to waste so much time on whippets and racing pigeons. When I warned you against the Never-Never system—that television set, that refrigerator. When I warned you——

EVERYMAN: But tha never did, luv. Tha encouraged me.

COMMON SENSE: You only heard me say what you wanted me to say. You dressed me up in your thoughts as Common Sense. At the same time you asked me to let my hair down. (*With one movement she releases a fall of hair. Then takes off her glasses and throws them to him.)* Here. Catch! Yes, you dressed me up as Common Sense. But underneath of course. . . . (*With one movement she unzips her frock and steps out of it, revealing very fancy bra and panties.*) I was your Wishful Thinking. (*She dances round Everyman.*)

EVERYMAN: *My* wishful thinking? My dream lass! (*He makes a grab at her: she eludes him.*)

COMMON SENSE: Everyman! That's no behaviour for somebody who's dying.

EVERYMAN: But ah've been coortin' thee for years. Isn't it time thee and me did summat practical about it?

COMMON SENSE: Time? Certainly not. No one can do those practical things with me. That is my nature, Everyman.

(*Gong.* EVERYMAN *pursues Common Sense round stage—? to music—and all but catches her.*)

DIRECTOR'S VOICE: Hold it!

FLOOR MANAGER: Hold it, both of you.

(EVERYMAN *and* COMMON SENSE *freeze in their tracks, he with his arms stretched towards her.* FLOOR MANAGER *approaches them.*)

FLOOR MANAGER. I'm afraid that's not allowed in this studio. Not while *I'm* Floor Manager.

(*He points to Exit.* COMMON SENSE *goes out.*)

(*To Everyman.*) You're forgetting this is a public entertainment. It's being watched by millions. Right, ready to go on?

EVERYMAN: Go on? Where to?

FLOOR MANAGER: Alex! Light Set One.

(*The luxury flat is lit up.*)

Jimmy, strike that picture. The one over the mantelpiece. Put the Picasso there instead of it.

JIMMY: The what, Morty?

FLOOR MANAGER: That picture leaning against the flat.

(JIMMY *holds it up.*)

JIMMY: This?

FLOOR MANAGER: That.

(JIMMY *hangs it on set.*)

And now that lump of stone with the hole in it, put it camera right. On that table.

(JIMMY *does so.*)

(*To Everyman.*) Take off that cap.

(EVERYMAN *takes it off. Wardrobe comes up and removes it.*)

EVERYMAN: Eee, lad, what dost want with me?

FLOOR MANAGER: You can take off that accent too.

EVERYMAN: Anything you say. What am I to play now?

FLOOR MANAGER: You're to play with your children, Everyman.

EVERYMAN: But which children? I've millions.

FLOOR MANAGER: Get on Set One. (*He points.*)

(EVERYMAN *goes upstage.*)

Now sit in that chair. Cross your legs and try to look rich.)

(EVERYMAN *does so.* FLOOR MANAGER *cues Son and Daughter, both expensively dressed, who come on and enter set.*)

EVERYMAN: Oh it's you! (*Uncrosses legs.*) You're too old to play with now.

SON: We were once too young to play with.

DAUGHTER: You *never* played with us, Daddy.

EVERYMAN: Absolute rubbish. I indulged your every whim.

SON: We didn't want them indulged. Why did you never

thrash me?

DAUGHTER: Why did you tell me I had talent when I hadn't?

EVERYMAN: Talent for what?

DAUGHTER: For painting.

EVERYMAN: But I thought you had.

DAUGHTER: Well, I hadn't. And you told me I didn't need training. You just threw that at my head. (*She points at the Picasso.*)

SON: Why did you let me come down after my first year at Oxford?

EVERYMAN: Because you wanted to.

SON (*bitterly*): Wanted to!

DAUGHTER: Why, when I was through with painting, did you let me go on the stage?

EVERYMAN: Well, you weren't on it very long, darling.

DAUGHTER: Naturally not. I was too bad.

SON: Why did you give me all that money when I came of age? That's why I never got anywhere.

DAUGHTER: Why did you consent to my marriage?

EVERYMAN: I couldn't have stopped you.

DAUGHTER: You encouraged me. And, since he was your junior partner, you must have known what he was.

EVERYMAN: I didn't, I didn't, I didn't!

SON: No, you never knew anything.

DAUGHTER: Which is why we don't know anything.

SON: We're out of touch with everything.

DAUGHTER: Even including ourselves.

EVERYMAN: I can't bear it. You're lying. My God, I did all I could for you. (*He rushes on to Set Two, which is still blacked out.*)

FLOOR MANAGER: Wardrobe!

(*A dresser dresses Son and Daughter in mackintoshes.*)
Set Two!
(*Set Two is lit up.* EVERYMAN *is sitting at desk.* SON *and* DAUGHTER *come in.*)

EVERYMAN: What do you mean? Coming into my office like this!

SON: This is the showdown, Father.

DAUGHTER: Yes, Father. This is it.

SON: I must have more money.

DAUGHTER: So must I.

EVERYMAN: But you've both got good jobs.

SON: I'm sacked.

DAUGHTER: I've turned in my chips.

EVERYMAN: It's not true!

DAUGHTER: It is.

SON: It is.

EVERYMAN: After all the education I've given you!

SON: *You've* given us! State scholarships.

DAUGHTER: And a fat lot of good they've done us.

SON: You promised us a brave new world——

EVERYMAN: It wasn't me; it was the State. You just said yourself it was.

DAUGHTER: I'd rather have left school at fourteen.

SON: So would I. I'd be somewhere by now. Instead of competing with the nobs——

DAUGHTER: And you can't compete with them anyway.

EVERYMAN: Look, it's nothing to do with me——

SON: That's just the point.

DAUGHTER: It never was.

SON: And that's why we want some dough from you.

DAUGHTER: It's the only reason we're here.

EVERYMAN: But . . . all this has happened before. *You* were sacked from *your* job, *you* resigned from *yours*—and you both came in here to dun me, wearing those very same mackintoshes. And I gave you a hundred quid each. Why put the clock back like this?

SON: Whose clock, Father? Yours—or ours?

DAUGHTER: We know about yours. It's stopping.

(EVERYMAN *runs on to Set Three.*)

FLOOR MANAGER: Dresser! Those teddy costumes. Quick.

(SON *and* DAUGHTER *are assisted in a quick change.*)

DIRECTOR'S VOICE: Camera One!

CAMERAMAN: Boss?

DIRECTOR'S VOICE: Track in on Set Three. Be ready for a tight three-shot.

(CAMERAMAN *raises hand and is pushed in towards set.*)

FLOOR MANAGER: Jimmy, got that cracked mirror in position?

JIMMY: Yeah, Morty.

FLOOR MANAGER: And what about the flick-knife?

JIMMY: He's got it.

FLOOR MANAGER: And she's got the lipstick?

JIMMY: Sure, Morty.

FLOOR MANAGER: Okay. Set Three!

(*Set Three is lit up.* EVERYMAN *is in bed under the bedclothes with only one shirtsleeved arm hanging out.*)

DIRECTOR'S VOICE: Hold it, Morty, till I tell you. Don't cue too soon.

FLOOR MANAGER: No, chief.

DIRECTOR'S VOICE: Grams! Put on that clock.

(*Heavy clock ticking on disc.*)

Try playing it faster.

(*Speed increased.*)

Okay. Right, Morty. Cue them.

(FLOOR MANAGER *cues.* SON *and* DAUGHTER *enter Set Three.* DAUGHTER *goes up to bed and peers.*)

SON: Ain't 'e croaked yet?

(*She shakes her head.*)

Bleedin' old crumb! See if 'is pocket book's under the pillow as usual.

DAUGHTER: See for yourself.

SON: Do as I tell you! You don't want the busies to catch us 'ere.

(*She puts her hand under the pillow.* EVERYMAN *grips her wrists and sits up.*)

DAUGHTER: Let go of me, you bleedin' old punk!

(SON *comes up and flashes flick-knife.*)

SON: Let go of her, pop, *or*. . . .

(EVERYMAN *drops her wrist.*)

That's more sensible. 'And me 'is pocket book.

(*She does so. He inspects it.*)

Yeah. That'll get us out of London.

EVERYMAN: So you'd rob your father!

SON: You don't need it no more. We do. The busies is after us.

EVERYMAN: Why, what you done this time?

SON: Done up an old party comin' out of the Ladies in the High Street.

DAUGHTER: The bitch! She must have spent 'er last penny down there. Nothing in 'er bleedin' 'andbag but a bleedin' lipstick. (*She takes it out of her pocket.*) Not such a bad one though. (*She starts to make up her mouth in mirror.*)

SON: Come on, Sis. You can do that later.

DAUGHTER (*still making up*): Trouble with you is you're yellow.

Director's Voice: Track in, One. Track in.

(*Camera moves in.*)

Everyman: 'Alf a tick. Leave me ten bob.

Son: Oh no we don't; you're dying. It's you what ought to be leavin' things.

Everyman: There's one thing I'll leave you. My curse.

(*Gong.*)

You brought nothing on me but disgrace. Pair of 'alf-baked delinquents.

Son: And 'oo was the one what 'alf-baked us. 'Oo was it failed to bring us up like?

Daughter: 'Oo was it told us everything was a racket? 'Oo was it told us to see to ourselves—once Ma died?

Director's Voice: Track in still further, One.

(*Camera pushes in.*)

Everyman: It wasn't my fault she died.

Son: I'm not so sure of that neither. But we ain't got time to argue that now.

(*Knocking by spot boy.*)

Daughter: Schtum! The busies!

(*Spot boy opens spot door.* Son *and* Daughter *swing round to face camera.*)

Floor Manager: Hands up, kids.

(*They both put up hands.*)

Director's Voice: Very nice shot, One. I'll just hold that a few seconds. (*Pause.*) Okay. Cut!

(*Set Three is blacked out.*)

Floor Manager: Elsie! Everyman's jacket! Jimmy! Rearrange that bed. And bring on the rocking-chair. (*Turns to audience.*) Well, ladies and gentlemen, I hope you're enjoying the show. I am anyway, even if you're not. Of course for me it's an ever-present problem; for you it's only a future problem. Talking of the future, have you heard the one about the three men in the crematorium? An Englishman, an Irishman, and a Jew. The argument was: who should be cremated first.

(*He is interrupted by* EVERYMAN, *staggering downstage.*)

EVERYMAN: The dice are loaded! The dice are loaded!

FLOOR MANAGER: Wait for your cue for speech.

EVERYMAN: I won't wait, I can't. I've got free will, haven't I?

FLOOR MANAGER: Not in this studio, chum.

EVERYMAN: But I'm Everyman; I've had millions of children. Those three pairs weren't typical. Think of John and Mary, Jean et Marie, Giovanni and Maria, Ivan and Marya, Sean agus Maire, Junior and Shirley. Think of all those Christmas stockings and yo-yos and Davy Crockett hats and toy pistols and national savings certificates and white mice and pop records and higher education and hula-hoops. Yes, more often than not I've been an excellent parent. Heaven knows that's true.

FLOOR MANAGER: *Heaven* knows? Eric! Move that boom over here.

(ERIC *swings the mike towards him.*)

(*Into Mike.*) Hullo there! Can you hear me? Only just? Then I'll raise my voice. Everyman—all right, I'll spell it. E for earth, V for virus, E for evil, R for ruin, Y for yellow, M for misfit, A for anguish, N for nobody. . . . That's right, Everyman. Well, Everyman claims he's been an excellent parent. . . . Excellent what? I'll spell it. P for pap, A for ashes, R for rot, E for envy, N for nonsense, T for torture: Parent. Everyman claims he's——

(*He is cut off by a burst of laughter through distort.*)

(*As laughter subsides.*) There you are, Everyman. That's your answer.

EVERYMAN: My answer? It's faked. Faked like everything else between these four walls. I'm walking out here and now. (*He moves towards one of the doors marked 'Exit' in lights, but as he reaches it, the two letters 'No' flash up to form the phrase 'No Exit'. He moves towards the other door, with the same result. All those in the studio burst into laughter.*)

DIRECTOR'S VOICE: Grams! Back up that laughter.

(*Add laughter on disc.*)

EVERYMAN (*coming downstage again*): Stop it! Stop it! Stop it! (*He puts his hands to his ears.*)

DIRECTOR'S VOICE: Okay. Grams out. (*The grams are cut.*)

FLOOR MANAGER: Stop laughing, chaps.

(*They stop. He goes up to* EVERYMAN *and gently removes his hands from his ears.*)

FLOOR MANAGER: Look, my dear fellow——

EVERYMAN: Take your hands off me. They're like ice.

FLOOR MANAGER: So are yours, my dear fellow. Not surprisingly. (*He looks at his wristwatch.*) Well, who's your next witness?

EVERYMAN: I've got no time for your so-called witnesses.

FLOOR MANAGER: Oh but you have. Though only a little time. Look, let me give you a tip. You're Everyman: it's in your character to get corrupted with the years. By the time you come on this floor you've forgotten the meaning of innocence. Suppose we go back to your youth?

EVERYMAN (*suddenly dreamy*): Yes. I was innocent then.

FLOOR MANAGER: Whom can you call on to prove it?

EVERYMAN: I know! My first love.

FLOOR MANAGER: Which of them?

EVERYMAN: Almost any of them would do. Jane, Joanna, Margot, Rosalind, Peggy, Patricia, Trixy, Sue; Ann-chen, Gretchen, Gretel, Greta; Ginette, Ninette, Babette, Colette; Francesca, Giovanna, Teresa, Lucre-zia——

FLOOR MANAGER: Okay, okay, point taken. Which do you choose?

EVERYMAN: Which . . . I leave it to you. First love is always genuine.

FLOOR MANAGER: All right then. Set Three!

(*Set Three is lit up. The bed has been converted into a settee with cheap cushions. A working-class girl sits in a rocking-chair, singing softly 'Rockabye Baby'. The dresser puts a cloth cap on* EVERYMAN.)

EVERYMAN: Doreen! (*He goes up on to set.*) Whatever were you singing that for?

DOREEN: I was looking ahead, Evvy, to when you and me get married.

EVERYMAN: Married?! . . . I'll have to wait for a rise.

DOREEN: Oh Evvy! You said last week——

EVERYMAN: I've thought it over since then. You see, Doreen——

DOREEN: I see only too well. It's that Connie with her perm and her giggle and——

EVERYMAN: It's not a bloody perm, it's natural.

DOREEN: So *it is* Connie! I knew it. (*She takes off a ring and hands it to him.*) Here, Evvy, take this back. It's cheap, it should just suit Connie.

EVERYMAN: But Doreen darling——

DOREEN: Don't darling me! There's the door; you needn't come darkening it again.

(EVERYMAN *hesitates, then goes downstage.* DOREEN *begins to sing again; her voice cracks as the lights dim. Set III is blacked out. The voice tails off, as the dresser removes Everyman's cloth cap and throws a college scarf round his neck.* MARY *comes downstage in a straw hat and a summer frock c. 1930. She approaches* EVERYMAN *from behind and tugs his scarf.*)

EVERYMAN (*turning*): Who's that? . . . Oh, Mary darling!

(*He pushes back her hat and they kiss.*)

MARY: What a wonderful day! I feel they've laid it on specially. Specially for you and me.

EVERYMAN: Who have?

MARY: Why, Those Ones. (*She points upward.*) Let's go and sit on the bank of the river.

(*They come right downstage and sit on floor facing the audience.*)

EVERYMAN: Look at all those mayflies. To think they live one day only!

MARY (*dreamily*): On a day like this . . . it might be worth it. I wonder . . . do mayflies have a love-life?

EVERYMAN: Of course they do. That's why they dance in the air so.

MARY: Everything's dancing today. Look at the ripple over there. And those willows going white in the sudden gust of wind. And that field of hay over there.

EVERYMAN: It isn't hay, silly; it's wheat.

MARY: Well, whatever it is, I shall never forget it. And why you should wear a scarf when the sun's as warm as this——! (*She removes his scarf and toys with it.*) That couple in the punt, do you think they're like us?

EVERYMAN: Certainly not. No one in the world's like us.

MARY: No one has the same world *we* have.

EVERYMAN: And no one has the same day we have.

MARY: No, I'll never forget this day.

EVERYMAN: I'll never forget how the sun at this moment brings out the lights in your hair.

MARY: Have you a hanky?

(*He shakes his head.*)

Pity. I was going to tie a knot in it. Never mind; this is even better. (*She ties a knot in his scarf.*) There! That's to remind you.

EVERYMAN: Of what?

MARY: Of me.

EVERYMAN: Oh you mug!

(*They embrace, then lie down interclasped.*)

DIRECTOR'S VOICE: Cue Forgetfulness. Track in Camera One.

(FLOOR MANAGER *cues. A female figure, wearing dark glasses, comes in and stands behind the couple, looking down on them.*)

DIRECTOR'S VOICE: A narrower lens, One. . . . Thank you. Nice composition.

(FORGETFULNESS *taps first Everyman, then Mary, on their shoulders.*)

FORGETFULNESS (*sadly*): Break it up, children; break it up.

(*They draw apart and stand up with their backs to each other.*)

MARY (*as if doped*): Where was I?

FORGETFULNESS: You were dreaming. (*She points to Exit.*)

(MARY *walks out as if sleep-walking.*)

EVERYMAN: I've been asleep. Was anyone here?

FORGETFULNESS: No one.

EVERYMAN: That's funny. I thought for a moment. . . .

(*He notices his scarf on the ground, picks it up and slowly*

unties the knot, then puts it around his neck.) What a horrible day! It's cold!
(*Gong.*)
(EVERYMAN *turns towards audience.*) And what am I doing by this river? Is it the Isis or the Avon or possibly even the Ouse or——

FORGETFULNESS: It's name is Lethe, Everyman.
She goes out while he stands gazing over audience.)

FLOOR MANAGER: Innocence, eh? You'd better go further back still.

DIRECTOR'S VOICE: That's right, Morty. Set up the Mother scene. Is she ready for her cue?

FLOOR MANAGER: She's been ready since we started.

DIRECTOR'S VOICE: Then cue her when you're set.

FLOOR MANAGER: Okay. I'll just check the props. Jimmy! Has she got the chocolates?

JIMMY: No, Morty. She hasn't.

FLOOR MANAGER: Then why the hell not? Give her those chocolates at once.

JIMMq: I can't. Somebody's eaten 'em.

FLOOR MANAGER: I'll talk to *him* later. What about the box?

JIMMY: Oh the box is okay.

FLOOR MANAGER: Then tie it up neatly with its ribbon. A big symmetrical bow, mind. Now where's that kiddy stool? You there, bring it down here.
(*A stagehand brings down a very small stool.*)

DIRECTOR'S VOICE: Two, can you hear me?

VOICE OFF (*on distort*): Yeah, boss.

DIRECTOR'S VOICE: In this scene you get an over-the-shoulder of Everyman. Three over-the-shoulder of the Mother. One does the two-shots. Clear?

(CAMERAMAN *raises hand.* FLOOR MANAGER *points to stool.*)

FLOOR MANAGER: Everyman! Sit there.

EVERYMAN: It's too small.

FLOOR MANAGER: I want it small. You're small too in this scene.

(EVERYMAN *perches very awkwardly on stool.*)

Okay. Look expectant. I'm going to cue your mother.

(*He raises his hand and after a pause, drops it.*)

(*The* MOTHER *comes in and rushes to Everyman whom she embraces; she is wearing Edwardian dress and carries a large box of chocolates and a book wrapped up in brown paper.*)

MOTHER: Evvy, my darling, my pet! Here's Mummy, back from her rest cure.

EVERYMAN: Oh lovely, lovely Mummy! It's been ages, it's been awful! Are you quite, quite better now?

MOTHER: 'Quite' perhaps, darling; not 'quite, quite'. But Evvy needn't worry; Mummy'll be 'quite, quite' soon. And she's brought some presents for Evvy. She got them the moment she left the rest cure place. First, there's this nice big book——

EVERYMAN: What's in that box, Mummy?

MOTHER: First there's this nice big book. (*She tears off the wrapping.*) I know my Evvy can't read yet so I got him a book full of pictures. There are stories in it too of course. They were written by a man called Hans Andersen.

(EVERYMAN *takes the book and turns the pages.*)

EVERYMAN: Ooh what's this? A Christmas tree!

MOTHER: That's right—but that's a sad story.

EVERYMAN: Why, what's sad about Christmas trees? Oh

here's a great big bird—it's a swan.

MOTHER: That's called the Ugly Duckling.

EVERYMAN: Why's it called a duckling if it's a swan? Ooh, I don't like this one! A little girl without any feet and her shoes are running away on their own.

MOTHER: That's another sad story. She was too fond of dancing.

EVERYMAN: But *you're* fond of dancing, Mummy.

MOTHER: Mummy won't dance again for some time, I fear. Ah, that's a man who lost his shadow. And this is a story called The Nightingale.

EVERYMAN: Who's that ugly big man looking over the end of the bed?

MOTHER: That's supposed to be Death. But don't be frightened; they sent him away.

EVERYMAN: Can anyone send Death away, Mummy?

DIRECTOR'S VOICE: Morty! You're in shot.

FLOOR MANAGER: Sorry, chief.

(*Having sidled in between the Mother and the camera, he now withdraws.*)

EVERYMAN (*shutting book*): Mummy, I don't like this book. Can I see what's in the box now?

MOTHER: Don't be impatient, my pet. I give you three guesses.

EVERYMAN: Chockies!

MOTHER: What a clever little boy my Evvy is. Yes, this box is as chockfull of chockies as . . . as Mummy's heart is full of love for her baby.

EVERYMAN: And Evvy's heart's full of love for his Mummy.

(*He embraces her and eagerly opens the box, which holds nothing but empty chocolate papers. As he drops them one by one on the floor, the lights dim gradually to blackout.*

A gong.)

DIRECTOR'S VOICE: Hold that blackout. Let her get off.

FLOOR MANAGER (*in darkness*): This way, Madam. Come with me.

(*In the darkness, off, a child's voice is heard singing a hymn as far as the lines*:

'Teach me to live that I may dread
The grave as little as my bed. . . .'

The voice is cut as the lights come up. EVERYMAN *is still sitting on the kiddy stool as if in a trance.*)

EVERYMAN: The grave . . . as little . . . as my bed? (*He slumps on to floor, in crumpled position, with face towards audience.*)

DIRECTOR'S VOICE: One, track in. And from above. Hold that shot. It's excellent.

(*Blackout stage and light up production gallery.*)

DIRECTOR: Excellent, isn't it, Pam?

SECRETARY (*in profile*): Yes, I think it's lovely.

DIRECTOR: And you, Julian?

DESIGNER (*in profile*): Beautiful foetal position. I'm sorry about the stool though.

DIRECTOR: Why, what's wrong with it?

DESIGNER: I specified something smaller.

DIRECTOR: Don't be perfectionist, Julian. That's a fault *I* grew out of long ago.

VISION MIXER (*in profile*): Shall I cut now?

DIRECTOR: No, hold it. (*On distort*). Morty! What about Sacrifice?

FLOOR MANAGER'S VOICE (*distant, on distort*): Sacrifice? She's just come in from make-up.

DIRECTOR (*on distort*): Okay. Stand by to cue her. But first get Everyman off that stool and strike it. One, get focussed on that entrance. Sacrifice will walk into camera. We'll lose Everyman for the moment.

VISION MIXER: You'll tell me when to cut?

DIRECTOR: The moment I say Cue. (*On distort.*) Ready, Morty?

FLOOR MANAGER (*on distort*): Ready.

DIRECTOR: Here we go then. Cue!

(*Blackout gallery, light stage.* EVERYMAN *is hidden behind a flat.* SACRIFICE *enters, dressed something between a nurse and a nun. She stands upstage and looks around.*)

SACRIFICE: I am Sacrifice. Does anyone want me? (*Silence.*) If nobody wants me, I will go back where I came from.

EVERYMAN (*rushing out*): No, no, no, don't go! You're my best witness—*my* Sacrifice.

SACRIFICE: You? Who are you?

EVERYMAN (*turning to audience*): Don't pay no heed to her, she's kidding. She knows me backwards same as I know her. Yes, she's the one'll speak up for me. Why, I've been in both her wars and not a conscript either. (*Dropping voice.*) Or sometimes I *have* been a conscript. (*Dresser puts on his head a World War I military cap.*)

DIRECTOR'S VOICE: Morty, cue Patria too.

(FLOOR MANAGER *cues.* PATRIA *enters, dressed like a synthesis of the Women's Auxiliary Forces. She stands beside Sacrifice.*)

EVERYMAN: Yes, I was at Mons, Gallipoli, the Somme, Passchendaele, the lot.

DIRECTOR'S VOICE: Come in, Grams.

(*'Tipperary' is heard off stage.* EVERYMAN *begins to march around stage,* SACRIFICE *following him.*)

EVERYMAN: I'm following you, Sacrifice, I'm following

you.

SACRIFICE: Are you, Everyman?

EVERYMAN (*still marching*): Only trouble is I can't see you. Which means I can't see the sense of you.

DIRECTOR'S VOICE: Cut grams!

('*Tipperary*' *ends abruptly.* EVERYMAN *comes to attention, facing Patria.*)

PATRIA: Everyman! Stand at ease.

(*He does so.*)

You know who I am?

EVERYMAN (*cockney*): 'Dulce et decorum est pro patria mori.'

PATRIA: Ten out of ten. Next question: why did you join up?

EVERYMAN: Because Kitchener pointed 'is bloody great finger at me.

SACRIFICE: You were patriotic in fact? You were true to *her*?

EVERYMAN: That's right. And true to you, too, ma'am. My Kitchener and country (*jerks thumb at Patria*) wanted me, and my sacrifice (*jerks thumb at Sacrifice*)—you was supreme!

PATRIA: You're lying, Everyman.

SACRIFICE: You're lying.

(PATRIA *removes his hat and extracts a large white feather.*)

PATRIA: *That* was why you joined up.

EVERYMAN (*to Floor Manager*): Now look 'ere, you're riggin' it again. I'm Everyman, I been millions o' different soldiers—not to mention sailors and airmen and Civil Defence and flamin' old National Fire Service.

FLOOR MANAGER: Dresser! Beret!

(*The dresser hands him a World War II beret.*)

DIRECTOR'S VOICE: Grams!

(*Air raid siren on disc: the Alert.*)

EVERYMAN (*educated voice*): Yes, World War Two. Dunkirk, Alamein, Anzio, Burma, Arnhem, what-have-you. In infantry, artillery, paratroops, tanks; in aircraft-carriers, submarines, corvettes, and minesweepers; as fighter pilot, navigator, rear-gunner, ground staff.

DIRECTOR'S VOICE: Wind him up, Morty.

(FLOOR MANAGER *makes winding-up movement.*)

EVERYMAN: But what's much more important than that—— (*He notices Floor Manager and breaks off.*)

DIRECTOR'S VOICE: That'll do. Grams. Lose it.

(*The 'Alert' fades.*)

PATRIA: Everyman! Shun!

(EVERYMAN *comes to attention.*)

Why did you join up this time? For me again?

EVERYMAN: No, not this time; of course not. The issues this time were international. King and country didn't come into it. All through the 'Thirties I'd been anti-Fascist and——

DIRECTOR'S VOICE: Hold it! Get Patria off.

(FLOOR MANAGER *cues Patria. She exits.*)

SACRIFICE: You were saying?

EVERYMAN: I thought this last war was a just one. I entered it for an ideal. And you, my Sacrifice, I thought you would be worth it.

SACRIFICE: And was I?

(*A pause: then the 'All Clear' is heard on grams.* EVERYMAN *throws his beret on the ground.*)

Was I?

EVERYMAN (*more to self*): All Clear they called it. . . . Nothing's clear.

(SACRIFICE *shakes her head sadly and moves slowly towards Exit.*)

DIRECTOR'S VOICE: Camera One! Hold Everyman, lose Sacrifice.

(*The All Clear fades out as* SACRIFICE *goes off.*)

Fine! Now, Morty, I think we'll have a break for tea.

FLOOR MANAGER: Relax all of you. We're giving you a break.

EVERYMAN (*cockney again*): Giving me a break, Guv? A break! When this whole flamin' show's been fixed and rigged and——

FLOOR MANAGER: Of course it's been fixed. It's a *permanent* fixture; it's popular. And there are plenty of people over there who'd be proud to be in your shoes. And, proud or not, they *will* be. Besides, I only meant a tea-break. (*To studio crew.*) Now listen, chaps, you've done pretty well so far but in the second half I want you all really on your toes. (*To audience.*) Ladies and gentlemen, we now have an interval. And I'd just like to remind you that after the interval we start with a few minutes' advertising. This will be in charge of the lovely little lady whom I introduced to you earlier.

(EVERYMAN *begins to light a cigarette;* FLOOR MANAGER *rounds on him.*)

Sorry, chum. (*He takes cigarette and stamps on it.*) Smoking forbidden in the studio—except when it's part of the action. And while I'm in charge of this floor—and I am and always shall be—— (*He turns to audience.*) . . . and that goes for all of you too—well, just remember I'm in charge. I cue you in and I cue you out. (*He strikes an attitude and begins to sing to the tune of 'John Peel'.)*

Oh I cue you in and I cue you out
And nobody knows what it's all about;
Though you start in hope you must end in doubt
When I knock on your door in the morning.

(*The studio crew have formed up behind him to constitute a chorus.*)

CHORUS:

Oh he cues you in and he cues you out
And nobody knows what it's all about;
Though you start in hope you must end in doubt
When he knocks on your door in the morning.

(BLACKOUT. INTERVAL)

ACT TWO

Lights come up on an empty stage. FLOOR MANAGER *walks on and blows a whistle. The hands pour on, making an enormous racket.*

DIRECTOR'S VOICE: Morty!

FLOOR MANAGER: Chief?

DIRECTOR'S VOICE: Stop that damned racket.

FLOOR MANAGER: Silence in the studio!

(*Silence.*)

DIRECTOR'S VOICE: Get her chalk marks, Morty?

FLOOR MANAGER: Chalk marks, Jimmy?

JIMMY (*pointing to floor*): Here, Morty. True to the centimetre.

FLOOR MANAGER: They're okay, Chief.

DIRECTOR'S VOICE: One on that entrance. Right, Morty. Cue Admom.

FLOOR MANAGER: Stand by all of you. The Admom cometh. (*He raises his hand, then drops it.*)

(ADMOM *enters to a fanfare, followed by a page carrying two hoops of different sizes—one for close-ups and one for middle shots—each shaped and proportioned like a TV screen.* FLOOR MANAGER *points her to her chalk marks.*)

ADMOM: Good evening, chickabiddies. Here is your very own Admom fresh from Salt Lake City. And she's brought her depth probers with her. (*She pulls out from her corsage two pencil-shaped surgical-looking instruments and points them playfully at audience.*) The very latest in motivational research. (*She hands the probers to a stage hand.*) You know the old saying of the famous British poet, Rabbie Burns? 'A chiel's amang ye taking notes.' Well, I'm not exactly a chiel—a child to you Sassenachs—after all I'm 38–24–38—but I certainly can take notes—*your* statistics are vital too—and I sure know my consumers. And talking of consumers, where's my little boyfriend, Everyman?

(FLOOR MANAGER *cues in Everyman.*)

Ah there you are, sweetie-pie! It seems an age since I told you about that cute new aperient. Has it had any effects yet? (*Without waiting for an answer, she turns back to audience.*) What other old friends do I see here? . . . Oh you honey! (*She waves towards back of audience.*) I'm glad to see you're wearing that invisible hearing aid. Well, you're certainly a peach of an audience—I only wish I could eat you. Old friends or new, I feel I know you so well. With all your little fads and human weaknesses—I guess it's because I'm maternal but I just adore those weaknesses. You there, sir, for example—— (*She blows a kiss.*) I know what *you* were up to today. Buying exactly the same things as usual—same brand of cigarettes, same brand of gin, same daily newspaper, same brand of peptalk—as you did yesterday and the day before yesterday and the day before the day before the day before yesterday, as you will tomorrow and the day after tomorrow and the day after the day after the day after tomorrow, or to cut a long story short what the dear old Romans called *in perpetuum*—and quite right too, I'm all for brand-consciousness. And you there, Madam, I must congratulate you. You went to the stores today, didn't you? What a fine example of impulse buying—it should be a lesson to all of us. Do let me know—if ever you get round to cooking it—what that canned nasturtium tastes like. And now, before we get on to our teeny-tiny concert—and don't expect any cha-cha, it will all be the dear old tunes that you learnt at Grandma's knee—I've a special word for Everyman. Come here and sit at my feet, honey.

(*He does so.*)

Everyman, to me you're just my Everybaby. This is a mass medium and you are my mass poppet. You are litmus paper and I am your acid or alkali. You are my hairy doormat and I am your highheeled shoe. You are my raw cloth; I am your tailor and cutter. You are my old flame; I am your brand-new bellows. You are my far-flung banner; I am your strange device. You are my horsepower; I am your chassis. You are my sweat-glands; I am your deodorant. You are my upper crust; I am your detergent. You are my holy spot; I am your holy spotlight. You are my stillborn child; I am your bottle of pickle. You are my lovely corpse; I am your lovely casket. In fact I'm your all-in-all—both tranquillizer and stimulant. You are my honey and I am your money. You my Admass and I your Admom!

(*She signals to page who hands her the smaller TV hoop which she holds up to frame her face, and begins to sing to tune of 'Comin' Round the Mountain'.*)

Oh 'tis I'm your second momma, Ev-ry-man,
'Tis I'm your second momma, Ev-ry-man,
'Tis I'm your second momma, I'm your second momma, 'tis I'm your second momma, Ev-ry-man.

(*The stage hands take up the chorus.*)

CHORUS:

Oh 'tis she's your second momma, Ev-ry-man,
'Tis she's your second momma, Ev-ry-man,
'Tis she's your second momma, she's your second momma, 'tis she's your second momma, Ev-ry-man.

ADMOM *singing*):

Oh 'tis I can soothe your fever, Ev-ry-man,
'Tis I can soothe your fever, Ev-ry-man,
'Tis I can soothe your fever, I can soothe your fever, 'tis I can soothe your fever, Ev-ry-man.

CHORUS:

Oh 'tis she can soothe your fever, Ev-ry-man,
'Tis she can soothe your fever, Ev-ry-man,
'Tis she can soothe your fever, she can soothe your fever, 'tis she can soothe your fever, Ev-ry-man.

ADMOM:

Oh 'tis I will gild your casket, Ev-ry-man,
'Tis I will gild your casket, Ev-ry-man,
'Tis I will gild your casket, I will gild your casket, 'tis I will gild your casket, Ev-ry-man.

CHORUS:

Oh 'tis she will gild your casket, Ev-ry-man,
'Tis she will gild your casket, Ev-ry-man,
'Tis she will gild your casket, she will gild your casket, 'tis she will gild your casket, Ev-ry-man.

DIRECTOR'S VOICE: Grams!

(*Outburst of clapping on disc.*)

In over it!

(FLOOR MANAGER *cues. A robot-like figure, like a deep-sea diver dressed in steel, with a huge steel head, various protuberant knobs and levers, and dials let into his chest, enters and stands beside Admom. Or he could be wheeled in on a trolley. The clapping fades.*)

ADMOM: Now here's an answer to *all* your worries. Everyman all through history—and Everywoman more recently—have wasted far too much time in the cumbrous business of thinking. But you needn't bother any more. Here is the very latest in infallible mechanical computers. Why be your own egghead when you can use electronics? (*She holds up the hoop to frame the Electronic Brain in a middle close-up. It points a lobster-like claw at audience and sings—in a metallic voice.*)

ELECTRONIC BRAIN (*singing*):

The old grey matter it ain't what it used to be, ain't what it used to be, aint' what it used to be,
The old grey matter it ain't what it used to be
Many long years ago—

CHORUS:

Many long years ago, etc.

ELECTRONIC BRAIN:

But I've taken over, I think on behalf of you, think on behalf of you, think on behalf of you,
I've taken over, I think on behalf of you
Now and for evermore.

CHORUS:

Now and for evermore, now and for evermore—
Oh, he's taken over, he thinks on behalf of us, thinks on behalf of us, thinks on behalf of us,
He's taken over, he thinks on behalf of us
Now and for evermore.

ELECTRONIC BRAIN:

Oh Adam and Eve hadn't heard of uranium, heard of uranium, heard of uranium,
Adam and Eve hadn't heard of uranium
Many long years ago.

CHORUS (*repeats*).

ELECTRONIC BRAIN:

So Adam and Eve were thrown out of Paradise, thrown out of Paradise, thrown out of Paradise,

Adam and Eve were thrown out of Paradise,
Many long years ago.

CHORUS (*repeats*).

ELECTRONIC BRAIN:

But Science today is the high road to Paradise, high road to Paradise, high road to Paradise,
Science today is the high road to Paradise,
Now and till Kingdom Come.

CHORUS:

Now and till Kingdom Come, now and till Kingdom Come,
Science today is the high road to Paradise,
Now and till Kingdom Come!

(*Clapping on disc. The* ELECTRONIC BRAIN *takes a bow and walks off, crossing* SEAN BULL *who briskly takes his place beside Admom.*)

ADMOM: And now—the famous Irish tenor, Sean Bull!

(*She holds up the hoop to frame his face. He sings in a mock sugary brogue, third-rate MacCormack, to the tune of* '*I'm sittin' by the stile, Mary*'.)

SEAN BULL (*singing*):

I'm sittin' on the fence, Mary,
Where we sat side by side,
When we did not know which way to go
For both our hands were tied.
Oh the trains I missed with you, Mary,
The dates that made no sense!
It all comes back to me today
Still sittin' on the fence.

(*Speaking without brogue.*) Buy Jedermann's super-galvanized fencing. It's unrustable, it's unbustable, it will save your hedging and trimming. All the top people use it. Jedermann's Super Fencing!

ADMOM: Thank you, Sean Bull. And your next?

SEAN BULL (*singing, again in brogue*):

Oh a power of black porter's flowed under the bridges
Of Shannon and Lagan and Liffey and Lee
Since Brian Boru slew the Danes in the ditches
And the bould Finn McCool courted Mother Machree.
But och the dear memories they rest evergreen
With a harp in the hand and a jar of poteen.

CHORUS: But och, etc.

SEAN BULL:

The green moon is settin' beyond the dark pylon
But still in ould Ireland the whiskey flows free,
With all the colleens wearin' stockin's of nylon
And Father O'Flynn rollin' down to the sea.
But och the dear memories they still linger on
Of Cuchullain and Deirdre and Potstill and Conn.

(*Speaking in brogue.*) Dhrink Irish whiskey—(*speaking in Scots*) when ye canna get Scotch.

(*Clapping on disc.*)

ADMOM: Thank you, Sean Bull; that was sweet.

(SEAN BULL *takes a bow and goes off, crossing Comedian got up like the early Chaplin.*)

And now—as our final titbit for tonight before I return you to your Master of Ceremonies. (*She looks at* FLOOR MANAGER *who bows.*) I have the greatest pleasure in introducing to you one of the best-known comedians of this country whose name is known to none of you for the simple reason that he's never himself. Tonight he is: Charles Chaplin.

(*Clapping on disc and out.*)

And, since he is the Chaplin of the early pictures, he

does not speak in his act. So on his behalf I will tell you his slogan. It is: 'Always carry a supercharged walking-stick.'

DIRECTOR'S VOICE: Morty! Where *is* his walking-stick?

FLOOR MANAGER: Jimmy. Walking-stick!

(JIMMY *runs down and hands Comedian a white stick. Instruments off strike up tune of 'The Moon Shines Bright on Charlie Chaplin'.* COMEDIAN *twirls his stick and shuffle-dances while* ADMOM *holds the larger hoop in front of him.*)

EVERYMAN: Coo, this takes me back!

(COMEDIAN *suddenly falls down.* EVERYMAN *runs up and assists him to his feet.* COMEDIAN *bows gravely to him and hands him the white stick.*)

COMEDIAN: You need it more than I do. (*He bows to audience and walks off briskly.*

EVERYMAN *passes his hand over his eyes and starts probing about with stick.*)

ADMOM: Everyman, honey! Can't you see?

EVERYMAN: No, Mom, Where are you?

ADMOM (*to audience*): Shows what suggestion can do. Everyman! Evvy! Come here.

EVERYMAN: Coming, Mom. (*He stumbles in the wrong direction.*)

She catches him up and steadies him.)

ADMOM: What happened to you, Evvy?

EVERYMAN: I was on the road to Damascus. (*Pause.*) Or was it the Dardanelles? (*He sings.*)

Oh the moon shines bright on Charlie Chaplin,
His boots are crackin'
For want of blackin'
And his little baggy trousers they want mendin'

Before we send him
To the Dardanelles.

ADMOM: Give me that stick.
(*He does so.*)
Now open your eyes.

EVERYMAN: But I can see!
(*She thrusts stick back into his hand.*)

EVERYMAN: No, I can't see.
(*She takes stick away again.*)
Yes, I can.
(*She thrusts it back.*)
No, I can't. (*He stands helplessly with both hands resting on top of stick.*
A dresser places on his head the Comedian's Chaplinesque hat which he had dropped in his fall.)

ADMOM (*to audience*): Nothing like a prop, is there? Which only goes to show that advertising's the eyesight of the nation. And your very own Admom here—why, she's also your very own optician. Not to mention a lot of things which rhyme with it. Your physician, your beautician—
(FLOOR MANAGER *makes winding-up sign.*)
Thank you, Morty—and your mortician too. Well, good night everyone; remember me in your dreams. (*She starts moving off.*
FLOOR MANAGER *snatches stick from Everyman.*)

FLOOR MANAGER: Here, take this with you. We want him to die with his eyes open.
(*She takes stick and walks to Exit, swaying her hips.*
EVERYMAN *fingers his eyes and addresses audience.*)

EVERYMAN: Who was that! I thought for a moment she was my mother. (*Pause.*) But, if she was, the milk was from a bottle.

ADMOM (*from Exit*): You're wrong, honey. It was dried milk. (*She goes out.*)

(*Gong.*)

FLOOR MANAGER: Elsie! Take away that hat.

(*A dresser removes the Chaplin hat.*)

Now let's get on with the action. Everyman, you're seeing all right again?

EVERYMAN: Yes.

FLOOR MANAGER: Sure?

EVERYMAN: Sure.

FLOOR MANAGER: Good. You'll need all the eyesight you've got. This is the green rub.

EVERYMAN: What does that mean?

FLOOR MANAGER: A naval expression: I learnt it off Singapore. The thin end of the wedge. You've still got to clear yourself, chum. Prove before you die that your life's been worth living. Prove that in your time you've not only taken but given. Prove that you've repaid your mother for her birth-pangs. Only this time perhaps you should choose your witnesses more carefully.

EVERYMAN: But I didn't choose them. I tell you the whole thing's been rigged.

FLOOR MANAGER: Did you hear that, Chief?

DIRECTOR'S VOICE: I heard. Never mind; we shan't cast him again.

FLOOR MANAGER: Everyman, get this straight. This is your only chance. And you ought to be proud that we gave you the chance. After all, you're only an amateur.

EVERYMAN: Amateur or not, I still say fair's fair. Why was I brought here in the first place if it's all a foregone conclusion?

DIRECTOR'S VOICE: Tell him: because we needed him.

FLOOR MANAGER: The Director says: because we needed you. *He* needed you—and *I* did.

EVERYMAN What for?

FLOOR MANAGER: You must find that out yourself. I can't give you all the answers.

EVERYMAN (*suddenly cockney*): No, I should say you can't! (*He walks downstage and addresses the audience.*) Tell you what it is, they've given me answers enough. And they've cooked 'em, I know they've cooked 'em; they're trying to make me a puppet. But I'm damned if they'll make me a puppet. I got free will, ain't I? Same as Napoleon and Christopher Columbus and the blokes that kept swimming the Channel.

FLOOR MANAGER: Who said *they* had free will?

DIRECTOR'S VOICE: Morty! Cue Free Will.

(FLOOR MANAGER *cues. A serious-looking man enters, in an overcoat and Anthony Eden hat, carrying a briefcase.*)

EVERYMAN: So *you're* the joker? Speak up for me.

(*Silence.*)

'Ere! Are you Free Will or ain't you?

FREE WILL: I am—but you never made use of me.

EVERYMAN: Oh didn't I! What about that time my dad ordered me into the factory and I ran away and got a job in a garage?

(FREE WILL *shakes his head.*)

(*Changing accent.*) What about the General Strike—in 1926, remember?—when I was a freshman at Oxford and I went against my class and served in a strikers' canteen?

(FREE WILL *shakes his head.*)

What about the time I offered a blood transfusion

when the other chaps held back?

(FREE WILL *shakes his head.*)

And the time I refused to agree to a divorce since I knew she'd come round—and she did?

(FREE WILL *shakes his head.*)

And the time I refused the Party Whip?

(FREE WILL *shakes head.*)

And the time that I volunteered for the N.F.S.?

(FREE WILL *shakes head.*)

And the time I stuck it out in the jury—four against eight we were but I swung 'em, my God, I swung 'em!

(FREE WILL *shakes head.*)

Well, if all you can do is shake your head——

FREE WILL: On none of those occasions can I remember that you called on me.

EVERYMAN: No?! Then how do you explain that——

FREE WILL: There are other people whose job it is to explain these things. Personally, I have another appointment. And I have to hurry: it's not on this planet. (*He takes off his hat to the audience and goes out briskly.*)

DIRECTOR'S VOICE: Morty! Set One. The Analyst.

FLOOR MANAGER: Eric! Set One.

(*Set One is lit up: it has been transformed into a psychoanalyst's consulting room. The* ANALYST *is waiting.*)

FLOOR MANAGER: Everyman! Up you go. Lie on that couch.

(*The* ANALYST *beckons.* EVERYMAN *goes up and lies on couch.*)

ANALYST: That's right. Close your eyes.

DIRECTOR'S VOICE: Track in, One, track in.

ANALYST: Now what is all this about free will? Nonsense, my child, those were all conditioned responses. The

Party Whip for instance—a simple Oedipus Complex.

EVERYMAN: Why?

ANALYST: Because you were in love with the Mother of Parliaments.

EVERYMAN: And the blood transfusion?

ANALYST: Oh blood: Blood for you represented the seminal fluid. In offering to give your blood to that man who'd just lost his legs, you were—in fact—committing an indecent assault on him.

EVERYMAN (*as if falling into trance*): Was I, father?

ANALYST: Yes, my child.

EVERYMAN: But the National Fire Service surely? I joined that simply because——

ANALYST: Simply because you wanted to *play* with fire. Your mother had always forbidden it when you were little.

EVERYMAN: So she had. There was the range in the kitchen and the open fire in the parlour—she put a big fender in front of that—and all of them lovely boxes of matches. Some of 'em had black heads and some had red but they all was out of my reach. And then there was spills for my father's pipe—the bastard!

ANALYST: You see? So when the Blitz came no fender was big enough for that. Naturally you joined the Fire Services; it was like going to a brothel.

EVERYMAN: Yes, I slid down the greasy pole and——

ANALYST: Ah that's another nice point——

EVERYMAN: And we drove on the bell and all the other bleeders made way for us. And the fires—the fires was so beautiful, jumping the streets like greyhounds and climbing the steeples like monkeys—and then there was all them miles of hosepipe——

ANALYST: Q.E.D. my child; Q.E.D.

EVERYMAN: I suppose so, father, but what about the jury? The time I swung them and got the chap acquitted.

ANALYST: Acquitted of what?

EVERYMAN: Funny. I can't remember.

ANALYST: If course you can't; you'd identified yourself with him. You knew he had done it, you see.

EVERYMAN: Done what, father, done what?

ANALYST: Done a little girl in the park. You were just becoming a dirty old man, so you couldn't convict a dirty old man. No, no, my child, free will doesn't come into it.

EVERYMAN: What does, then, father?

ANALYST: I do.

(*He places his hand on Everyman's forehead.*)

And you know what I'm going to do now? I'm going to remove all these complexes of yours so that you can start again from scratch. With an absolutely clean sheet.

EVERYMAN: A clean sheet?

ANALYST: A blank mind.

EVERYMAN: How long will it take?

ANALYST: Depends on your resistance. Not less than three or four years; it might take ten or twelve. I'll have to go deep, you know.

EVERYMAN: I can't spare the time. I can't spare the time. I'm dying.

(*Set One is blacked out and Set Two lit up. It has now become a classroom. The* MARXIST *places a blackboard on an easel and turns round, rapping on his desk with a pointer.* EVERYMAN *comes in.*)

MARXIST: Comrade, you're late for my lecture.

EVERYMAN: Why? I can't see anyone else here.

MARXIST: Of course you can't, you're Everyman. You *are* everyone else.

DIRECTOR'S VOICE: Camera One, a narrower lens. I want a close-up of the blackboard.

(MARXIST *indicates blackboard, which is blank, with pointer.*)

MARXIST: Now what does this represent?

EVERYMAN: I can't see anything. It's blank.

MARXIST: It's only blank to one of your bourgeois mentality. Follow my pointer. (*Without touching the board he describes a rapid complicated pattern just in front of it.*) That . . . is the dialectic!

EVERYMAN (*as if doped*): Oh the dialectic? Of course, Comrade.

(*The* MARXIST *turns the blackboard round. Its other side is equally blank.*)

MARXIST: Now here are the axioms. Can you read them?

(EVERYONE *stares blankly, then takes out spectacles and puts them on.*)

What does it say here about freedom?

(EVERYMAN *takes off his spectacles and shuts his eyes.*)

EVERYMAN (*patly*): Freedom is the recognition of necessity.

MARXIST: You're coming on, Comrade. That clause in our creed must never be forgotten. But how does it apply to you, Comrade? Think of your past actions. What about that time you worked in the strikers' canteen?

EVERYMAN: When was that?

MARXIST: 1926.

EVERYMAN: Oh yes, the General Strike; I was a freshman at Oxford. The other undergraduates I knew were helping to break the strike. They were true to their class in fact.

MARXIST: While you . . . were untrue to your class?

EVERYMAN: Yes.

MARXIST: But why?

EVERYMAN (*parrotwise, with no expression*): I was untrue to my class, not because I really saw the light—I had not even read *Das Kapital*—nor yet because I was in any way capable of choosing between good and evil—I mean revolution and reaction. It was merely that in me, or rather in my family and social background, the disease of capitalist morality had reached an even further point than in most of the other undergraduates. I was an Honourable, you see, while most of *them*, well, they weren't even Etonians. My heritage then was an abscess and as such it had to burst. I just *had* to throw in my lot with the strikers; I did so adore doing anything unconventional. Apart from that, of course, it was an absolute necessity.

MARXIST: But you did not then recognize it as such?

EVERYMAN: Didn't I, my dear fel-, Comrade?

MARXIST: When you went to serve in that canteen, you thought you were acting freely?

EVERYMAN: Of course I did.

MARXIST: So you weren't. You had been utterly conditioned by history, you just had no choice in the matter. If you had known you had no choice, then you'd have been free—one of us. But you *thought* you had a choice, so you weren't free. And, even though you joined us, you weren't one of us. Q.E.D., Comrade?

EVERYMAN: Q.E.D., father.

MARXIST: Right. Come up here. Take this chalk. I want you to draw a diagram.

EVERYMAN: Diagram of what?

MARXIST: Of the future.

EVERYMAN: The future? I don't know what it's like.

MARXIST: I said you weren't one of us! Give me back the chalk and I'll show you. (*He draws a large circle on the blackboard.*) This is the earth. (*He draws a hammer and sickle within the circle; then draws a smaller circle.*) This is the moon.

(EVERYMAN, *in hypnotic excitement, snatches the chalk.*)

EVERYMAN: I get it! I get it! (*He marks the moon with a hammer and sickle, then turns the blackboard round and draws a huge circle almost filling it.*) This . . . is the sun!

(*He is about to draw in the hammer and sickle when the* SCIENTIST *enters from Set 3.*)

SCIENTIST: Everyman! You're going too far. That's completely unscientific. You can't make the *sun* a satellite. Even your friend here can't. It's a contradiction in terms.

MARXIST: Comrade, I'd thank you not to interrupt my lecture.

SCIENTIST: A thousand apologies. I thought this was a seance.

MARXIST: A seance?

SCIENTIST: Well, you know; blackboard-turning. You've put Everyman there in a trance.

MARXIST: He came to me in a trance.

(SCIENTIST *looks at his watch.*)

SCIENTIST: Well, your time's up anyway. I'm taking over now. Come with me, Everyman. (*He takes his arm.*)

MARXIST: How dare you! You rotten deviationist!

SCIENTIST: Deviationist? No, Comrade, Scientist.

MARXIST: Then as a scientist you must know that you

yourself are conditioned, that the whole of science is conditioned by——

(*The* SCIENTIST *whips out a large syringe.*)

SCIENTIST: I'll condition you!

MARXIST (*backing away*): What's that?

SCIENTIST: Just a little injection. To change your personality, Comrade.

MARXIST: But I haven't got a personality. The personal cult's been exploded.

SCIENTIST: Never mind; this will change what you *have* got. You won't be a Marxist any more.

MARXIST (*appalled*): I won't be a. . . ?!

SCIENTIST: Certainly not. You'll be even more of an automaton. You think you're the master? I am! (*He chases* MARXIST *and jabs him in the behind.*) There!

MARXIST (*wailing*): Ooh! And my best trousers too! My best trousers! (*As he rubs his behind, his expression turns imbecile.*)

DIRECTOR'S VOICE: Camera One! Lose Marxist. Follow the other two.

(SCIENTIST *conducts Everyman on to Set Three which has now become a lab; on a table is a large microscope.*)

SCIENTIST: Now, Everyman. What is this?

EVERYMAN: Looks like a microscope.

SCIENTIST: Correct. Come over here. I'm going to put you under it.

EVERYMAN: What!

SCIENTIST: When I say 'you' the word 'you' of course is an abstraction. A convenient concept that has no basis in fact.

EVERYMAN: You mean I've no basis in——

SCIENTIST: The word 'you', the word 'I', all such words

are meaningless. Why, you might as well start using a word like 'soul'.

EVERYMAN: But I do use the word 'soul'.

SCIENTIST: My dear fellow! We're not in the Middle Ages. Come on, it won't bite you, have a peep.
(EVERYMAN *looks into microscope.*)
Well, what do you see?

EVERYMAN: A lot of raspberry jam. Only it's moving about.

SCIENTIST: That's what you're made of, Everyman. Just a moment, I'll change the slide. (*He does so.*)

EVERYMAN: Little things wriggling and squirming.

SCIENTIST: That's what you came from, Everyman. And what your children all come from. In the bed you were thinking of 'love'—another meaningless word—but that's what it all was really. Now let's go a little further. (*He changes slides again.*) That is a cell.

EVERYMAN: A prison cell?

SCIENTIST: Yes, in a manner of speaking. There are millions on millions on millions of those inside you and yet Everyman himself, in a sense, is a prisoner in each of them. (*He changes slides.*) That . . . is a gene. The primary living particle. That's what conditions Everyman's life—the long arm of heredity.

EVERYMAN: It doesn't look like an arm; it looks like two spirals intertwining. How big is this thing really?

SCIENTIST: We're down to molecular level. So are we here. (*Changes slide.*) That is a virus. It has certain things in common with a gene.

EVERYMAN: I thought a virus was a disease.

SCIENTIST: If it is—so what? Maybe all life is a disease. After all think of cancer. A cancer is a growth—and life is a growth. On the other hand what you are looking at— and it's part of you, Everyman, it's a part of you—may not be alive at all. The interesting thing about a virus, the fascinating thing, is this: we just don't know what it is. It may be a micro-organism, it may be merely a chemical. Though I should apologize for saying 'merely': the organic world has no right to sneer at the inorganic; the minerals after all are the chaps that are going to outlast the lot of us. But to return to our virus: it seems to be somewhere on the border—the border of life and non-life. Which suggests of course that life can be reduced to non-life.

EVERYMAN: You're telling me!

SCIENTIST: *I'm* telling you.

DIRECTOR'S VOICE: Morty! Get out of shot!

(FLOOR MANAGER *draws away from in front of the camera.*)

SCIENTIST: And now for the next slide.

EVERYMAN: You can keep your next slide; and you know what you can do with it! (*He pushes the microscope over.*)

SCIENTIST: That will cost you——

EVERYMAN: Send the bill to my undertaker. And as for your billions of cells, I'm going to break out of one and all of them. I'm not taking this lying down.

SCIENTIST: You're going to lie down very soon.

EVERYMAN: In the body maybe, but my soul——

SCIENTIST: Oh that thing again!

EVERYMAN: I believe in that thing, I tell you. Whatever you say, I am I. There *is* such a person as myself.

SCIENTIST: Yourself? Well, go and look for it.

EVERYMAN: I will. (*He turns his back on the Scientist and*

strides downstage.)

DIRECTOR'S VOICE: Fine so far. Hold it.

FLOOR MANAGER: Hold it all of you. Very nice work, the three stooges; now we'll line up the musical. Bert, bring that stand-mike down.

(BERT *does so.*)

Okay. Downstage please the Scientist, the Marxist, the Analyst. Now you needn't use much voice. Just mind your diction.

(*The Three stand round the mike, ready to sing in turn.* FLOOR MANAGER *cues the Analyst.*)

ANALYST: (*singing*):

I'm gonna probe probe probe your dark subliminals,
Uproot each secret that the Censor hid,
Gonna wean you clean from your own personality,
Gonna take away your Ego and leave you with your Id.

THE THREE:

Take away your Ego and leave you with your Id.

MARXIST:

I'm gonna lick lick liquidate your memory,
Gonna save you from the sty of the bourgeois swine;
You must change your old beliefs for a suit of dialecticals
And hang out your washing on the Party Line.

THE THREE:

Hang out your washing on the Party Line!

SCIENTIST:

I'm gonna scroot scroot scrutinize your elements,
Gonna take you, baby, cross the Great Divide
Down among the molecules ——for in the last analysis
Life is just a drop of dirty water on a slide.

THE THREE:

Just a bloody drop of dirty water on a slide!

(FLOOR MANAGER *joins them at the mike.*)

FLOOR MANAGER:

I'm gonna cue cue cue you to your destiny,
Gonna brief you and groom you to embrace your bride,
But the wedding bed is narrow and smells of chrysanthemums
And Everyman who gets there finds he's died.

THE FOUR:

All of you who get there will find you've died!

(*Flourish on an instrument.*)

EVERYMAN: My self! My self! Where can I find my self?

(*He roams round stage.*)

VOICES OFF:

Not here, Everyman. Not through the microscope.
Not through the telescope.
Not through the spectroscope.
Not on the highways or byways.
Not in the dark of the womb.
Not in the gaps in the galaxy.

ANALYST (*approaching Everyman*): Good-bye, my child.

MARXIST: (*following*): Good-bye, Comrade.

SCIENTIST (*following*): Good-bye, specimen.

(*All three hold out their hands;* EVERYMAN *refuses and turns his back on them.*)

EVERYMAN: I turn my back on the three of you—(*he looks at* FLOOR MANAGER)) and on you also. I will talk to my fellows who *don't* know all the answers. (*He comes downstage and addresses audience.*) 'Moriturus te saluto.' That's what the doomed gladiators cried out in Ancient

Rome to the Emperor. 'I who am about to die salute you.' But in *this* arena I say it to you, to each of you. (*He looks searchingly in different directions over the audience.*) Moriturus te saluto. Moriturus te saluto. Moriturus te saluto. I did not choose to be put in this ring to fight, I did not ask to be born, but a babe in arms is in arms in more senses than one and since my birth I've been fighting. Conscript or volunteer—I just don't know which I am—and it may have been a losing battle but at least I've been in it, I've been in it. And *les jeux sont faits* and *rien ne va plus*. To be a human being is a cause for grief—and for pride. Everyman must vindicate himself. Oh I know they say one has no choice in the matter, but I don't believe them. Do you? Caddy! Where's that caddy?

(*The* CADDY *runs on with the huge golf-bag.*)

My driver!

(CADDY *gives him a driver. He tees up an imaginary ball, takes a few practice swings, then drives it over audience.*)

There! I can't see if it's on the fairway or not but at least it carried. (*He passes the driver to a stage hand.*) Now my sweep's rods.

(CADDY *hands them over—a three-piece set.* EVERYMAN *fits them together and lunges upwards.*)

Yes, as I thought. A filthy chimney. I've been cleaning it as long as I remember, but the soot comes back again quickly. Compounded of doubts and megrims and all the malaise of our time. (*He lunges upwards again, then ducks as if to avoid a fall of soot.*) Never mind, that's better. I've earned my sweep's wages, I think. (*Same business.*) Next.

(CADDY *hands him a large stone-breaker's hammer.*)

'M. Working on the roads again. (*He takes a swing.*) Breaking stones—like when I came out of Eden. (*Swings.*) There were no roads then. I had to start from scratch. (*Swings.*) And then there was Stonehenge. (*Swings.*) And Troy—and Memphis—and the roads of Rome. (*He leans on the hammer.*) Stones! I've broken 'em by the million, but they've never broken *me*. (*He hands over the hammer.*)

CADDY: And now, sir?

EVERYMAN: Now . . . my conductor's baton.

(CADDY *hands it to him.*)

DIRECTOR'S VOICE: Morty! Wind him up.

(MORTY *makes winding-up sign.* EVERYMAN *ignores him.*)

EVERYMAN: If I cannot conduct my life, at least I'll conduct my death. We'll start with the last movement. (*He raises the baton.*)

DIRECTOR'S VOICE: Wind him up, I said.

FLOOR MANAGER: Sorry, Chief. He won't look at me.

(EVERYMAN *begins conducting but is immediately interrupted by some stage hands who burst in, carrying a large rocket—Thor model perhaps—in three parts.*)

DIRECTOR'S VOICE: Hold it! Hold it! What's *that*?

FLOOR MANAGER: Hold it all of you. I don't know, Chief. I'll find out. What the hell sort of prop is that, chaps?

HAND: A rocket of course. And it's practical. Easy there with the warhead.

FLOOR MANAGER: He says it's a practical rocket.

DIRECTOR'S VOICE: Well, I didn't order rockets. It must be for the show next door. They've got extra firemen laid on there.

FLOOR MANAGER: Sorry, chaps; you're in the wrong

studio. Take that pretty little toy next door. It's a show called 'No Man and His Future'. You know, just one more documentary.

HAND: Okay, Morty; sorry about the mistake. But I naturally thought, seeing *you* was the F.M. here——

FLOOR MANAGER: Oh I'm the F.M. there too. It doesn't come on till tomorrow; get me?

HAND: I get you Morty. Okay, chaps, take it away.

(*As they carry it out the* CROONER *runs in and grabs the stand mike.*)

CROONER:

'I'm just a rock rock rocket in the dark,
Intercontinental!
Interplanetary!
Interuniversal!
Just a rock rock rocket that will pop pop pop!

CHORUS: (*Repeats. Then instrumental coda.*)

DIRECTOR'S VOICE: Okay, Morty. Blackout while they strip him for action.

FLOOR MANAGER: Action?

DIRECTOR'S VOICE: His last.

FLOOR MANAGER: Wardrobe! Make-up! On your toes! Quick change here for Everyman. After that, duckies, you can relax. Okay, all lights out.

(*Studio is blacked-out but Gallery is lit up dimly to show the backs of Director and his associates in black silhouette. None of them moves. A voice begins to sing from the darkness.*)

SINGER:

There's a long long trail a-winding
To the land of the tomb
Where the mocking bird is singing
And the long shades loom,

Where your eyes all turn to blindness
And the world all turns to stone
And Everyman must walk along
That long long trail alone.

DISTANT CHORUS: (*Repeats.*)

(*Then Gallery is blacked-out, and lights come up slowly on stage to show* EVERYMAN *in loincloth, medievally emaciated; make-up girl is putting last touches to his face.*)

DIRECTOR'S VOICE: One. Give me a close-up. 'M. Not enough sweat.

FLOOR MANAGER: Lil, can you get him more sweaty?

LIL: I'll try, Morty.

FLOOR MANAGER: Cold sweat, remember. Deathbed stuff.

LIL: That better?

FLOOR MANAGER: That better, Chief?

DIRECTOR'S VOICE: Middling. Never mind, I'll close for it. Right, we'll run the next sequence.

FLOOR MANAGER: Stand by all of you. We're just about to——

DIRECTOR'S VOICE: Hold it! Where's that damned tomb?

FLOOR MANAGER: Jimmy! What the devil are you up to? We've not got all night for this job. Bring on that tomb at once and——

JIMMY: Not my fault, Morty. The painters are still finishing the graining of the marble——

FLOOR MANAGER: To hell with the graining of the marble! We needn't be all that naturalistic. Wheel the wretched thing on; can't you see Everyman's shivering?

(*The tomb is wheeled on upstage; it is in the form of an allegedly marble oblong box about three feet high with a foot-stone and a headstone. A stage hand slaps a 'sticker' marked 'Wet Paint' on the footstone and another marked 'Vacant', on the headstone.)*

DIRECTOR'S VOICE: Looks all right; the viewers will think it's marble. Okay, cue the Gravedigger.

(FLOOR MANAGER *cues. The* GRAVEDIGGER *enters, an impressive bearded figure carrying a spade. He stands behind the headstone, resting his crossed arms on it.)*

DIRECTOR'S VOICE: Right. Now the guard of honour.

FLOOR MANAGER: Bill! I can't see the chalk-marks.

BILL: Here they are, Morty.

(FLOOR MANAGER *traces the chalk marks—nose to ground.)*

FLOOR MANAGER: I see . . . but why do they go zigzag?

BILL: That's to allow time for the Recessional.

FLOOR MANAGER: Bright boy. (*He pats Bill on the head.*) Right. Now we line up the Guard of Honour. In the following order. Career and Common Sense—there are your chalk marks.

(CAREER *and* COMMON SENSE *take up their positions downstage facing each other.)*

Sacrifice and Patria!

(*They do the same upstage from the first pair.*)

The Comedian and the Brain!

(*Same business.*)

And four volunteers, please. (*Pause.*) Come on. Anyone who's got nothing better to do.

(*He beckons to some of the stage hands who come sheepishly forward. Gradually the complete guard of honour, in two rows of five couples each, is lined up, running diagonally upstage from stage L. to R.*)

STAGE HAND (*from back of guard*): Don't we have no words, Morty?

FLOOR MANAGER: No, this isn't a wedding. But you're

right, you've got to do something. Try this. (*He holds up his arm in the Nazi salute.*)

(*The guard of honour do likewise.*)

FLOOR MANAGER: Does that fill the bill, Chief?

DIRECTOR'S VOICE: No.

FLOOR MANAGER: Try this then. (*He raises the Communist clenched fist.*

Guard of honour follows suit.)

DIRECTOR'S VOICE: No, no, no——

FLOOR MANAGER: What about this? (*He extends his arms upwards and outwards, with palms together, in a praying gesture.*)

(*The Guard of Honour do the same, suggesting an abortive arch.*)

DIRECTOR'S VOICE: 'M. That takes me back. Okay, I'll close for that.

FLOOR MANAGER: Okay chaps, keep it like that. Now Everyman—where have you got to? (*He looks down.* EVERYMAN *is lying at his feet.*)

FLOOR MANAGER: You've collapsed a shade too soon, chum. Can't you get up?

(EVERYMAN *shakes his head.*)

All right; do it on your belly then. And follow what I tell you. This is your Guard of Honour. Or, putting it another way, your Northwest Passage. You must pass up—crawl up—between these two ranks till you get to the bourne from which—you know the rest of the quotation?

EVERYMAN: I won't. I'm not going!

FLOOR MANAGER: No?

EVERYMAN: No, I tell you. Never!

FLOOR MANAGER: Never's the operative word. (*He points.*)

This is the road to Never. And I'm the Floor Manager here and I'm cueing you up that road.

(*He cues* EVERYMAN *who, as if hypnotized, begins to crawl up the passage formed by the Guard of Honour. He crawls slowly in stylized jerks in time with the music. When he reaches the end of the Guard they reform in a second diagonal running stage R. to L., and then in a third L. to R. which will bring him almost to the tomb. Meanwhile the Recessional has been sung—tune 'Comin' thro' the Rye', taken very slow, as a dirge, and possibly punctuate with a muffled drum or tubular bells.*)

SINGERS:

'Gin a body miss his body
Comin' thro' the Rye,
Gin a body lose his body
Need a body die?
  Oh Everyman he also ran
  He also ran sae fast,
  But when his ghost had reached the post
  It found its chance was past.
Gin a body miss his body
Comin' thro' the Rye,
Gin a body lose his body
Need a body die?
  Oh a' ma life was storm and strife
  And yet I lo'ed it well,
  But what it meant or where it went
  I fear I canna tell.
Gin a body miss his body
Comin' thro' the Rye,
Gin a body lose his body
Need a body die?

(*A great bell tolls once.* EVERYMAN *has emerged, still on his belly, from the passage formed by the Guard.*)

FLOOR MANAGER: Guard of Honour! Hands to your sides! Dismiss! (*They march off.*)

(*Simultaneously two professional-looking gentlemen, dressed alike as if they were twins, walk on from different sides and stand over Everyman. One is the* DOCTOR OF MED, *one is the* DOCTOR OF DIV.)

MED (*to Floor Manager*): Is this my patient?

(FLOOR MANAGER *nods.*)

DIV: My patient, you mean.

FLOOR MANAGER: You can share him between you. Who will examine him first? The Doctor of Med or the Doctor of Div?

MED: We'll toss. You call.

DIV: No, I'll toss. (*He spins a coin.*)

MED: Ladders.

DIV: Snakes. Everyman, get on your feet. (*He helps him up.*)

FLOOR MANAGER: Chair, Jimmy.

(JIMMY *places chair on to which* EVERYMAN *subsides.*)

DIV: Now to business. What is your name?

EVERYMAN: M or N.

DIV: Who gave you this name?

EVERYMAN: Some bastard, I suppose, who'd come down from the trees.

DIV: Did you have no name before that?

EVERYMAN: Before that? When?

DIV: Well, shall we say in the era of the giant reptiles. Dinosaur, diplodocus, ichthyosaurus, pterodactyl.

EVERYMAN: I'm sorry . . . I can't remember.

DIV: Or before that again? When everyone lived in the sea.

EVERYMAN (*dreamily*): Did I live in the sea? . . . Yes, of

course I did. Things were much easier then.

DIV: And who was it put you in the sea?

EVERYMAN: Don't know.

(DIV *pulls a Bible from his pocket.*)

DIV: You don't know! Have you never read this?

EVERYMAN: What is it? I'm blind.

DIV (*reads*): 'And the earth was without form, and void; and darkness was upon the face of the deep.'

EVERYMAN: Yes. This is where I came in. 'Here beginneth the last lesson.' 'It is written . . . it is written——' I can't remember.

DIV: It is written: ye shall not grow young as angels and songs grow young. Nor shall the hand move back on the dial nor the cord that was cut be joined. For man is contracted to his doom as the lemming swimmeth to the west. And the ravens croak in Lover's Lane and the telephone is not answered.

EVERYMAN: But after that?

DIV: A board is raised with the words 'To Let' and the board is removed again and Everyman's place is filled and his latchkey changed and the papers in his desk skimmed through and thrown in the basket and burnt.

EVERYMAN: And I myself?

DIV: Have you faith?

EVERYMAN: How can I tell?

DIV: Then how can *I* tell either? *If* you had faith——

MED: He hasn't? My turn now, my dear fellow.

DIV: You're welcome. See you in the club. (*He walks off.*)

MED: Now, Everyman. I was going to say open your shirt but I see you haven't got one. (*He pulls out a stethoscope and examines him.*) Yes indeed. As I thought. You're a walking hospital. You were always dead on the surface; now you're dying in the depths.

EVERYMAN: I was always dead on the surface?

MED: Of course: think of your skin. Everyman's skin is a dead rind. Which means that all that we see of him is dead. For his hair's dead too, you know. (*He picks up Bible which Div has dropped, opens it absently, then closes it.*) It is written: What is man that the beasts should respect him save that he walketh upright, whereby his arches fall and the discs come loose in his spine and his guts press on his pelvis? And though he live longer than most—yet not so long as a tortoise—his bones grow brittle and his skin wizened and his arteries harden and his glands degenerate and his brain turns bad. Yes, Everyman, you've not come to me one moment too soon.

EVERYMAN: You mean you can save me?

(*Gong.*)

MED: Save you? Of course not. But I can start straight away to write your certificate.

EVERYMAN: But can't you do anything for me? A blood transfusion? . . . A life transfusion?

MED: A forlorn hope—but I'll check. There *might* be some life donors present. Don't die before I come back. (*He walks downstage looking towards audience and singing. This lyric should be set like a slow Negro Spiritual.*)

MED (*singing*):

Is there a life donor here,
Oh is there a life donor here,
Like Elijah was to the widow's child—
Is there a life donor here?

CHORUS:

No, there ain't no life donor here,

There ain't no life donor here,
We got enough to do to keep ourselves alive,
Oh there ain't no life donor here.

MED:

Is there a life donor here,
Is there a life donor here,
Like Ezekiel was in the valley of bones—
Oh is there a life donor here?

CHORUS:

No, there ain't no life donor here,
There ain't no life donor here,
Them bones gotta stay in the valley of bones
For there ain't no life donor here.

MED:

Is there a life donor here,
Is there a life donor here,
Like Pasteur was when the rabies came—
Oh is there a life donor here?

CHORUS:

No, there ain't no life donor here,
There ain't no life donor here,
We'd give it away if we'd got it to give
But there ain't no life donor here.
(*Rallentando.*) There ain't no life donor here.
(MED *has returned upstage to Everyman.*)

MED: I'm sorry. They're all the wrong group.

GRAVEDIGGER (*still leaning on headstone*): Come on, Everyman. I'm waiting.

MED: Right. He's all yours. (*He walks off.*)

(*At the same time* FREE WILL *and* CONSCIENCE *enter from opposite sides.*)

GRAVEDIGGER: Come on, Everyman.

EVERYMAN: I can't. I'm blind. Where are you?

(FREE WILL *and* CONSCIENCE *take each an arm.*)

CONSCIENCE: Come with us.

EVERYMAN: Who are you?

CONSCIENCE: I am your conscience. I have returned to you.

EVERYMAN: And you?

FREEWILL: I am your free will.

EVERYMAN: You exist then?

FREE WILL: I do. Now let's go. One step at a time. That's the way. Easy does it.

(*They take* EVERYMAN *as far as the footstone.*)

CONSCIENCE: Lean on this.

EVERYMAN: You're not leaving me?

FREE WILL: Don't worry; you're in good hands.

EVERYMAN: Whose hands?

GRAVEDIGGER: Mine.

(FREE WILL *and* CONSCIENCE *stand aside, but stay watching.*)

EVERYMAN: Who are you? My father? You sound like him. Not entirely though: you sound kinder.

GRAVEDIGGER: Do I? Thank you.

EVERYMAN (*feeling footstone*): What's this? The foot of a bed?

GRAVEDIGGER: Yes, the foot of a bed.

(*Children's voices, distant, are heard singing—without words—the hymn-tune* '*Teach Me to Live*'.)

Everyman, time's nearly up. Before you get into bed would you like to say your prayers?

EVERYMAN: I would—but I can't remember any.

GRAVEDIGGER: Supposing I help you?

(*The singing ends.*)

Repeat the lines after me. O Thou whoever Thou

art——

EVERYMAN: Thou whoever Thou art——

GRAVEDIGGER: And whether Thou art or not——

EVERYMAN: Whether Thou art or not——

GRAVEDIGGER: To Thee I make mine avowal——

EVERYMAN: To Thee I make mine avowal——

GRAVEDIGGER: I, Everyman, stand here alone——

EVERYMAN: I, Everyman, stand here alone——

GRAVEDIGGER: Having sinned against life and myself——

EVERYMAN: Having sinned against life and myself——

GRAVEDIGGER: But before I leave this world——

EVERYMAN: Before I leave this world——

GRAVEDIGGER: O Thou whoever Thou art——

EVERYMAN: Thou whoever Thou art——

GRAVEDIGGER: I thank Thee for giving me the chance——

EVERYMAN: I thank Thee for giving me the chance. (*Pause.*)

GRAVEDIGGER: If I failed to use it, forgive me.

EVERYMAN: If I failed to use it, forgive me.

GRAVEDIGGER: And now: ten seconds silence.

FLOOR MANAGER: Ten seconds silence in the studio. (*Silence. The* FLOOR MANAGER *cues* GRAVEDIGGER *who comes and puts his arm round Everyman.*)

GRAVEDIGGER: Time for bed, Everyman. I'll help you in——

EVERYMAN: But who *are* you?

GRAVEDIGGER: Who am I? Most people think I'm the end but I am also the beginning. I was present when your mother bore you. Can you feel how strong my arms are? (*He moves* EVERYMAN *away from footstone.*)

FLOOR MANAGER: Everyman, don't hold your head up. You're supposed to be——

GRAVEDIGGER: Stop it, Morty. You needn't listen to *him* any more. Every hour of your life he's been standing at your elbow and whispering, or breathing down your neck—and his breath has always been cold. But now at this hour of your death—that's right, hold your head up—it's I who call the tune. Everyman, here and now, I salute you in the name of Life.

EVERYMAN: And *your* name?

GRAVEDIGGER: I've just said it. And now, Everyman, relax.

(*He lifts him and places him in the tomb.*)

(*Blackout. Children's voices are heard singing, without words, the tune of* '*Happy Birthday to You*'. *As they end, the* DIRECTOR'S VOICE *is heard.*)

DIRECTOR'S VOICE: Okay, Morty. Lights!

FLOOR MANAGER: Lights, Eric!

(*The studio is lit up. The* GRAVEDIGGER *removes the label* '*Vacant*' *from the headstone.* FLOOR MANAGER *comes downstage to address the audience.*)

FLOOR MANAGER: Well, ladies and gentlemen, that's it. As I warned you, this show was really more like a rehearsal. For Everyman, for me—and for you. And Everyman, remember, was only an amateur. As I imagine most of you are. So please don't be too critical of his performance. If it were you in his place, well, I'm sure you'd like the benefit of the doubt. That's all. Good night. Thank you. (*He turns and joins the* GRAVEDIGGER *and shakes hands with him; then gives him his headphones.*) There you are, chum. The next show's yours.

GRAVEDIGGER (*having put on the cans*): Hullo, Chief! Can you hear me?

DIRECTOR'S VOICE: Perfectly. Your voice is clearer than

Morty's. Okay. Cue the Finale.

GRAVEDIGGER: The 'Finale'?

DIRECTOR'S VOICE: Call it anything you like. Call it a Prelude if you want to. But cue it, my dear fellow, cue it.

GRAVEDIGGER: Okay. Chorus formation! Stand by everyone—Everyman. (*He picks up baton and conducts, as the lights turn very dim.*)

CHORUS (*to tune of 'Tannenbaum', slow*):

Oh Everyman, oh Everyman,
Behold we weep for Everyman.

SOLO:

So few the suns that rose and shone
Before the dark fates moved him on.

CHORUS:

Oh Everyman, oh Everyman,
We bid farewell to Everyman.

(*The tune changes to 'The Road to the Isles'.*)

SOLO:

The blind Fury is loose upon the land
And every man and woman is her slave,
The blind Fury 'tis she that holds our hand
As step we down the highroad to the Grave.

CHORUS:

By Loch Failure and Loch Sorrow and Loch Evil we must go
Where the storm clouds are brooding on the wave
For whatever else we know not there is one sure thing we know:
We must all take the highroad to the Grave.

(*The lights gradually get brighter and the tempo becomes much faster.*)

Solo:

The bright daylight is here for all to see
Whatever it may mean of storm and strife,
The new freedom we shall find when we are free
And the chance of each man's lifetime is his life.

Chorus:

By Loch Sunlight and Loch Moonlight and Loch Lovelight we may go,
And our heart beating fast as drum and fife,
For whatever else we know not there is one sure thing we know:
That the great chance of your lifetime's your life.

Chorus:

Oh Everyman, oh Everyman,
We wish new joy to Everyman.

Solo:

Joyful returns of life on earth,
Each day he lives a day of birth!

Chorus:

Oh Everyman, oh Everyman,
A new day dawns for Everyman.
(*Instrumental coda and blackout.*)

A few notes based on the first production at the Abbey Theatre Dublin, October 1966.

(1) The first act should be played at the tempo of a revue, thus keeping up the element of surprise and effecting a contrast with the 2nd Act (though 'Admom' must also have the tempo of revue).

(2) The first song 'On Earth for What It's Worth . . .' has no tune. A young actor at the Abbey, Des Cave, improvised one. All other tunes are traditional—English, Scottish, American and Irish (except 'I'm just a rock rock rocket').

It is recommended when translating songs to set them to the traditional tunes of the country concerned, unless a tune is so-well known as to be common property, e.g. 'O Tannenbaum'.

(3) Page 75. ('Everyman begins conducting but is immediately interrupted by some stage hands who burst in, carrying a large rocket. . . .')

At the Abbey this was accompanied by the Chorus dancing in and singing the Crooner's song 'I'm just a rock rock rocket in the dark'. (Tune by Gerald Victory.) It had the effect of speeding up the action and worked very well.

All songs were vamped with two electrical guitars and a drum ensemble.

HEDLI MACNEICE